Bricks and Stones from the Past

Bricks and Stones from the Past

Jamaica's Geological Heritage

Anthony R.D. Porter

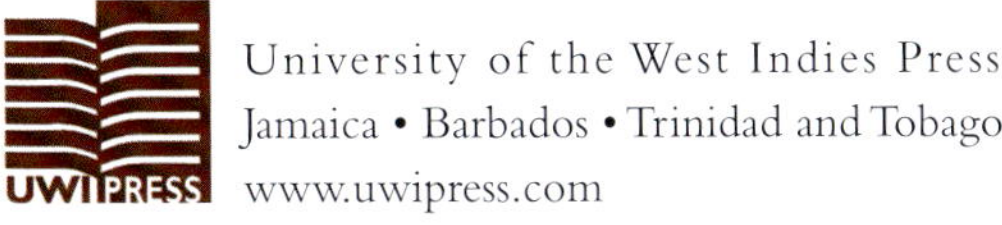
University of the West Indies Press
Jamaica • Barbados • Trinidad and Tobago
www.uwipress.com

University of the West Indies Press
7A Gibraltar Hall Road Mona
Kingston 7 Jamaica
www.uwipress.com

10 09 08 07 06 5 4 3 2 1

CATALOGUING IN PUBLICATION DATA

Porter, Anthony R.D.
Bricks and stones from the past: Jamaica's geological heritage / Anthony R.D. Porter.

p. cm.

Includes bibliographical references.

ISBN-10: 976-640-192-6
ISBN-13: 978-976-640-192-4

1. Architecture – Jamaica. 2. Building stones – Jamaica. 3. Historical buildings – Jamaica. 4. Jamaica – Buildings, structures, etc. I. Title.

NA809.P78 2006 720.97292

Book and cover design by Robert Kwak.

Set in Bembo and Frutiger.

Printed in Canada.

Dedicated to the memory of our ancestors – black, brown and white; free men and women, indentured servants and slaves; skilled artisans and merchants, sailors and soldiers, and others – who were responsible for the production of the objects and structures described in this book. Let us honour your sacrifices by preserving them for future generations.

Contents

Illustrations

Figures

Plates

Tables

Preface

In 1997, a chance meeting in Kingston with Raymond Brandon, a retired businessman, former student of Jamaica College, and longtime member of the Jamaican Historical Society, led to the unexpected renewal of an earlier interest that I had in archaeological and historical sites. I had long been aware that much of the island's early development was based on the use of imported stone for buildings and other purposes. Some of these stone types and their uses had been briefly described in two previously published books – *Minerals and Rocks of Jamaica* (1982) and *Jamaica: A Geological Portrait* (1990). But it was Raymond who made me aware that there were many other stone artefacts and objects all over Jamaica, many in private collections and some at the Institute of Jamaica, about which little was known. And so began another of my many undertakings – this one being to carry out a meticulous research of the written records (especially the fourteen large Journals of the House of Assembly of Jamaica housed at the National Library in Kingston), and simultaneously re-explore the whole island in search of imported and local stone used either in construction or for other purposes.

To appreciate the magnitude of the task, it is important to bear in mind that when the British forces invaded Jamaica in 1655 and captured the island from the Spaniards, the country was underdeveloped. But in the 1700s, especially during the latter half of the century, the production and export of sugar rapidly transformed it into one of the most prosperous small islands in the world. One of the legacies of this period is the large number of skilfully built structures that sprang up all over the island – notably aqueducts, bridges, churches, fortifications, great houses, sugar factories, tower mills and walls. The material used in their construction depended on the availability of suitable locally occurring stone. Consequently, most were built of white limestone (which is widespread and abundant throughout much of the island), often in combination with bricks and lime mortar. But an interesting variety of other stones and bricks were also transported to Jamaica in sailing ships from England, Scotland, Ireland, Wales, Italy, Barbados and other countries and used in the development of the island. Then in 1907 the island was rocked by a severe earthquake which did extensive damage island-wide. Immediately thereafter a new building code was formulated; reinforced concrete was introduced into Jamaica, bringing to an end the island's five-hundred-year dependency on brick and cut stone for construction purposes.

Given the ever-growing interest in heritage tourism and the need for more readily available information on the island's stone artefacts and early building stones, I decided in early 2001 to disclose the extent of my research in the form of a lengthy address to members and friends of the Jamaica Historical Society. The talk, entitled "Imported and Local Stone Use in Pre-1900 Jamaica", was published later that year in their regular bulletin. In the continued spirit of information sharing, much of the text contained in chapter 6 was reprinted by the society in volume 11 (2003), while chapters 3 and 5 were released to the Institute of Jamaica for publication in the *Jamaica Journal,* volumes 27 and 28 (2004).

This book, however, while including most of the basic information reported in those publications, contains much more in the way of an expanded text as well as numerous maps, diagrams, tables and photographs. It is intended as a guide for anyone interested in knowing more about Jamaica's rich geo-heritage, and the role played by brick and stone in the development of the island up to the turn of the twentieth century. Hopefully, work now in progress by researchers in the fields of archaeology, geology and history will provide answers to some intriguing questions that beg for closure.

Anthony R.D. Porter
Mandeville, Jamaica

Acknowledgements

While researching and writing this book, I came into contact with many individuals who were profoundly helpful, and my sincere appreciation is extended to everyone who contributed along the way. But I owe a special debt of gratitude to the late Raymond Brandon, who, in addition to being a friend and touring companion, was a tremendous source of information, and without his assistance and encouragement this book would probably not have been written.

A special word of thanks must also be extended to a host of others – some with whom I had many fruitful discussions, and some of whom either graciously allowed me to examine artefacts in their possession or granted me permission to examine historic structures on their properties. Those I have chosen to single out are – in alphabetical order – as follows: Ronald E. Anderson (retired geologist, Mandeville); the late Tony Clarke (Paradise Park, Westmoreland); Ronald Coleman (retired marine archaeologist, Queensland, Australia); Stephen K. Donovan (former professor of geology, University of the West Indies); Eleanor Douglas (Falmouth, Jamaica); Peter Francis (architect and built heritage preservationist); Michael Gardner (head, Department of Anatomy, University of the West Indies); Robert G. Garrett (scientist emeritus, Geological Survey of Canada, Ottawa); A. (Tony) Goffe (prospector); Sheila, Tony and Blaine Hart (owners and operators of Good Hope estate in Trelawny); Leeta Hearne (retired editor); Alex Henderson (owner of Orange Valley estate, Trelawny); the late

W. (Billy) Hopwood; the late W. (Billy) Ives; Trevor A. Jackson (professor of geology, University of the West Indies); Phillip Alsworth-Jones (senior lecturer in archaeology, University of the West Indies); Wynne Jones; Mary Langford (historian); George Lechler (civil engineer and historian) and his son, James Lechler; Wendy Lee (environmentalist); Frank Lohmann (owner of Shafston estate, Westmoreland); Graham K. Lott (geologist, British Museum); Trevor McCain; Alfred Morrison; Stephen D. Porter (London, England); Rosie Ridgeway (Port Royal); Edward (Ted) Robinson (professor emeritus, Department of Geography and Geology, University of the West Indies); Gordon H. Sabiston (retired geochemist, Kingston, Ontario, Canada); Jacky Shepard (Miami, Florida); Dorothy and the late Howard Shirley; David Smith (geologist and curator, The Natural History Museum, London); Thomas Stemann (lecturer in Geology, University of the West Indies); Stephen Solomon (antiques valuator); Sorena Sorensen (Smithsonian Institution); R. (Bobby) Stockhausen (businessman, Kingston); the late G.E. (Ted) Tatham; Eulalee Thompson (The Gleaner Company); Rona (Molly) Wade (Port Royal); Mona Webber (senior lecturer in life sciences, University of the West Indies); and Robyn P. Woodward (archaeologist, Simon Fraser University, British Columbia, Canada).

It is also a pleasure to gratefully acknowledge the technical assistance of the following organizations and certain members of staff: Alcan Jamaica Company (especially the laboratory expertise of Desmond Lawson and Ram Viswanathan); the Jamaica Archives in Spanish Town; the National Library of Jamaica (especially Tenshia Armstrong); the Institute of Jamaica and its Archaeology Division (particularly Michael Cooke, former director of museums, and Wayne Modest, the current director); the Jamaica National Heritage Trust (especially Roderick Ebanks, Evelyn Thompson and Karleen Williams, all based in Kingston, and Joan Seagers at Seville Heritage Park in St Ann); the Mines and Geology Division at Hope Gardens (in particular Georgette D'Aguilar); the Department of Correctional Services (especially Superintendent Sylvester Lindo, formerly stationed at Fort Augusta); and the Ministry of Environment, Energy and Natural Resources in Barbados (in particular Ingrid Blackman and Leslie Barker).

All illustrations are the work of the author (unless otherwise identified) and were digitally scanned by Tropicolour, a subsidiary of Lithographic Printers Limited in Kingston. Sincere appreciation is extended to them as well as to SGS Mineral Services in Toronto, Canada, for carrying out some of the analytical work reported here.

I am also deeply indebted to the ever-helpful University of the West Indies Press team, under the guidance of Linda E. Speth, general manager, and Shivaun Hearne, managing editor, for taking up the challenge of sailing out into uncharted waters, and to Claudette Upton, copy editor, for wading through and painstakingly correcting the writings of a geoscientist.

And, finally, my fondest thanks to my immediate family, Joan, Gordon and Kristina, for their patience and support.

1

Introduction

Wherever we travel on land we are sure to see clay and soil in fields and on hill slopes; sand, gravel and boulders in bank sides, in river and stream beds and along the coast; and bedrock exposed in cliffs, road cuts and quarries. In general, all of this material is composed of substances called minerals. There are some three thousand known species of mineral, but only about seventy are common, and these make up most of the rocks that form the Earth's crust. Yet, despite our dependence on minerals for adornment, modern conveniences, weapons and other essential tools, most people know very little about them.

Scientifically speaking, a mineral is defined as a naturally occurring chemical element or compound formed as a product of inorganic processes, whereas rocks are aggregates of one or more minerals (just as words are composed of one or more letters). Rocks are further classified, according to mode of origin, into igneous, sedimentary and metamorphic. To have a thorough understanding of minerals and rocks it is necessary to undertake intensive investigations of them both in the field and laboratory, and this requires many years of work.

But there are a few simple tests that can help the amateur identify minerals and rocks. Each mineral has a characteristic chemical composition, crystal form and set of physical properties. Certain substances, for example, will leave permanent marks on glass, whereas others can be easily cut by a knife blade. The resistance of a substance to scratching or abrasion is called hardness, which is one of the most practical properties used in mineral identification. In 1812 a German

Mineral	Hardness	Common Tests
Talc	1	Scratched by a fingernail, hardness 2.5
Gypsum	2	Scratched by a fingernail, hardness 2.5
Calcite	3	Scratched by a copper coin, hardness 3.5
Fluorite	4	Scratched by a knife blade, hardness 5.0
Apatite	5	Scratched by window glass, hardness 5.5
Feldspar	6	Scratches a knife blade and window glass
Quartz	7	Scratches a knife blade and window glass
Topaz	8	Scratches a knife blade and window glass
Corundum	9	Scratches a knife blade and window glass
Diamond	10	Scratches all known minerals

Table 1.1 Mohs Scale of Hardness

mineralogist named Friedrich Mohs developed a scale of ten common minerals in order of increasing hardness. Known as the Mohs Scale of Hardness, it is still widely used. Each mineral in the scale will scratch the one numerically below it, and minerals with the same hardness will scratch each other. Thus, gypsum will scratch talc and be scratched by calcite. Hardness can also be determined with the use of other objects, as shown in Table 1.1.

Another useful property is the substance's reaction to the application of dilute hydrochloric acid (HCl) or vinegar (acetic acid) to its surface. All carbonate minerals, notably calcite ($CaCO_3$), will instantly begin bubbling or effervescing; dolomite ($CaCO_3$ $MgCO_3$) will effervesce to a lesser degree. As most readers know, Jamaica is an island with a hilly to mountainous interior, bordered on the south side by an expansive alluvial coastal plain. Located in the Caribbean Sea, the island has a surface area of 4,400 square miles (11,400 square kilometres), approximately 60 per cent of which is composed of limestone. The acid test, therefore, is of the utmost importance in mineral identification.

When the Tainos (formerly called the Arawaks) arrived in Jamaica (around AD 600–650), the vegetative landscape was vastly different from the way we know it today. At that time the land was largely forested, and most of the food plants that we take for granted were not here. While it is believed that the Tainos brought cassava, maize (corn), arrowroot and sweet potatoes, we know for certain that there were no oranges, bananas, plantain, coconuts or sugar cane – as these were subsequently brought to the island by the Spanish. But most of the materials that they needed to manufacture utensils and tools were obtained from the loose rock and mineral matter occurring in abundance in riverbeds and on the plains, especially on the south side of the island.

During British colonial rule the tradition of importing food crops continued, with the introduction of ackee, breadfruit, coffee, mangoes and other plants. Building materials were also brought from overseas for a variety of purposes. Then, in 1907, the city of Kingston and other parts of the island were badly damaged by an earthquake. This event marked a turning point in the construction industry, as the building code was changed and reinforced concrete introduced. Significant historical events that have shaped Jamaica and led to its development since the arrival of the Tainos are listed in the appendix.

In recording the past, historians, archaeologists, geologists and others have often tended to work independently of each other. One of the drawbacks of this approach is that important details are sometimes overlooked, often leading to either a distortion or an incomplete historical account of a people, place or structure. A re-examination of the island's artefacts, built heritage and historical records reveals that the different peoples who have inhabited Jamaica from the early seventh century have used minerals and rocks in a variety of ways, which can be subdivided into four main categories.

POTTERY

Pottery is a utilitarian or decorative ware made from baked (fired) clay. This practice dates back thousands of years, and pieces ranging from simple pots and bowls to sophisticated works of art with intricate patterns and designs have been found at many sites around the world. The four basic steps in making pottery are preparing the clay mixture, shaping it, decorating and glazing it, and firing it in an oven. In general, three types of pottery are recognized – earthenware, stoneware and porcelain. Earthenware is a common pottery made by baking a mixture of clays at low temperature. This method can produce bright, colourful glazes, but the resulting pottery is more easily chipped and broken than other types of pottery. Terra cotta (literally, cooked earth) is a hard, generally unglazed, reddish-brown earthenware commonly used for vases, jars, flowerpots, roof tiles, gutters, figurines, statues, sculptures and assorted utilitarian vessels (flasks, pots, bowls, griddles).

Pottery made by the aboriginal Tainos has been found at numerous midden sites all over Jamaica and includes clay implements of various kinds, made in open hearths. In general, the vessels are usually circular or boat-shaped (often with handles), rounded at the base, unglazed and characterized by surface markings or indentations such as straight parallel lines, dots or W-shaped lines around the rim. Archaeologists have divided the remains into two types – Redware and White Marl. Redware is the older type and refers to the highly burnished potsherds, or broken pieces, and complete vessels often characterized by anthropomorphic and zoomorphic designs. The more recent White Marl pottery is simpler in form and was not fired using red slip (that is, coating the outside of the object with a weak mixture of water and clay). Yabbaware is a general term used to describe heavy, sometimes glazed earthenware vessels (bowls, pots, monkey jars and so on) manufactured in Jamaica by people of West African origin. These vessels were initially fired in open hearths and later in kilns.

Another type of pottery that has been found in Jamaica is called Majolica. This is a soft, porous white earthenware pottery, whose surface is uniformly covered by an opaque tin oxide. It is most commonly decorated in blue, but other metallic oxides are used to produce various colours and designs. Majolica pottery was introduced to the New World by the Spanish explorers, and in Jamaica it has been recovered from a few early-sixteenth-century occupation deposits, notably Sevilla Nueva,[1] White Marl and Spanish Town.

Archaeological excavations of the Old King's House site in Spanish Town have also uncovered olive-jar sherds and fragments of other European earthenware, as well as red-clay tobacco pipes similar to those brought up at Port Royal by Robert Marx in 1966–67. According to Mathewson, "Olive jars were never much over eighteen inches high, and oftentimes had a green glaze over a dull pink to tan fabric. The distinctive collared neck is most characteristic of the seventeenth and eighteenth centuries."[2] The larger storage vessels, commonly called Spanish jars, are later in origin. They are easily recognized by their bright-orange to reddish-brown colour, distinctive shape (tapering from top to bottom), large size (just over 3 feet or 1 metre in height) and other features such as two arc-shaped ridges and the presence of an insignia, logo or crest. These jars, however, were manufactured in the Tuscany region of Italy and were brought to the island by the British, not the Spanish.[3]

Two other types of earthenware that have been found are Delftware from the Netherlands and Faience from France. The latter is glazed with tin oxide to produce a creamy white colour. Various hues, however, can be obtained with other metallic oxides.

Stoneware is a hard, heavy, impermeable ceramic made by baking a mixture of special clays at very high temperatures. Since the heat generated during firing causes the surface to become glossy, it is not necessary to glaze the objects. Popular stoneware items include containers for storage, durable dishes, pipes, statues and other objects. Both stoneware and earthenware are opaque.

Porcelain (also called chinaware) is a hard, white, usually translucent (in thin edges) pottery made by baking a mixture of kaolin (or china clay) and China stone (composed mainly of a silicate mineral called feldspar). There are three main kinds of porcelain: hard-paste, soft-paste and bone china, the latter so called because bone ash is added to the mixture. Fragments to complete pieces of factory-manufactured pottery, ranging from Wedgwood (Queen's Ware) to Chinese porcelain, have been recovered from the site of the Old King's House in Spanish Town.

BRICK

Brick is an oblong or rectangular block made of clay, crushed shale and other materials. It is the oldest manufactured building material, having been used as long ago as 6000 BC. Many different civilizations produced brick by hand-shaping or moulding blocks of clay and mud and drying them in the sun. Although this method continues in some of the more remote parts of the world, today most bricks are manufactured by machines and fired (baked) in large kilns or ovens. During the Middle Ages, the period in European history extending from about AD 400 to 1500, brickmaking declined in England owing to changes in architectural styles and the availability of wood and stone. In Jamaica, the Spanish had begun construction of Sevilla Nueva (just west of the present town of St Ann's Bay) in 1509 and manufactured bricks locally for that purpose. The original remains of these were discovered by accident in subsurface brick-lined wells on the Seville estate in 1938.[4]

The arrival of the British in 1655, however, signalled the demise of all structures built during the Spanish occupation. Some were destroyed by the Spanish themselves and the rest by the invading British forces – in any case, nothing was left standing above ground. Then in 1666, disaster struck in London, England, in the form of a "Great Fire", which raged for three days and destroyed many wooden buildings. This led to a resurgence in brickmaking and the use of bricks for house construction.

Meanwhile, the construction of Port Royal and the reconstruction of Spanish Town had been using thousands of bricks imported from England, along with local hardwoods for doors, roofs, windows and ceiling beams. But in 1692 a devastating earthquake rocked Jamaica, doing great damage. Part of the town of Port Royal slid into the sea, and attention was immediately turned to building a new city known as Kingston. In the nineteenth and twentieth centuries, diving expeditions to explore the sunken section of Port Royal discovered a trove of artefacts, bricks and other building stones.

Over the years historians and others, in describing various ruins and buildings of historical interest in Jamaica, have neglected to record some of the important details. To state that a building is made of red brick leaves many questions unanswered. In addition to recording a structure's dimensions, the historian should note the bricks' texture, colour and (if present) the manufacturer's insignia, initials or logo, because in the eighteenth and nineteenth centuries bricks were made locally (chiefly in Kingston and Spanish Town) for building purposes, as noted in the following passages from the *Journal of the Assembly of Jamaica*:

> A petition of James Reily, of the parish of Kingston, brick-maker, was presented to the house, and read, setting forth "That, in the months of March and April, 1782, the petitioner did deliver, at his brick-kiln in the said town of Kingston (by the express orders and command of Thomas Keating, esquire, the commanding officer in the district of Kingston), 38,800 good and sufficient bricks, for the purpose of carrying on the public works at Port-Royal, as appears by the certificate of the said Thomas Keating, hereunto annexed."[5]

Meanwhile, at the other end of the island, it was reported that 116,000 bricks were among the goods that had "entered inwards at the port of Montego Bay, from the kingdom of Ireland; from the 1st day of November, 1785, to the 1st day of November, 1786".[6]

Another important observation to make is the way in which bricks are laid. In general, they are placed horizontally in layers, called courses, and the bricks are bound together with mortar, the composition of which often differs from place to place and building to building. Today, most mortar is a mixture of Portland cement, lime, sand, gravel and water. But before the advent of cement in Jamaica, the early builders used various mixtures consisting of lime, sand and water (producing a milky-white mortar) or bauxite, lime, and water, sometimes with the addition of sand, molasses or straw (producing a red-brown or yellow-brown mortar). Such mixtures are very cohesive and can bind bricks together for hundreds of years. Mortar also prevents moisture from seeping through the walls.

For structural reasons, bricks are staggered so that the vertical joints do not coincide with each other. This permits the weight and pressure to be distributed over a greater area. The bricks are also arranged in patterns called bonds – that is, they are laid with either their short or long ends exposed. The St John Anglican church at Guanaboa Vale in St Catherine is a good example of a red-brick structure in which each course is made up of alternating long ends (called stretchers) and short ends (called headers). This pattern is known as Flemish bond (see chapter 2). Another feature that should be recorded is the degree of coarseness or fineness of the brick. A close inspection of many old buildings will reveal that not only the colour but the grain size of the bricks varies, with some being fine and even-textured, others gritty and coarse (Plate 1.1).

Plate 1.1 Coarse-grained bricks with slate damper. Old Naval Hospital, Port Royal.

A semi-quantitative chemical analysis of a small selection of bricks manufactured by the Spanish and the British is shown in Table 1.2.

NATURAL BUILDING STONES

Building stone is the general term applied to any natural rock formation that is used as a construction material. It is extracted from the Earth's surface by quarrying, and the material is removed either in a crushed or broken state (hence the term *crushed stone*), or cut into large blocks and slabs to specific dimensions (dimension stone). Today, crushed stone or aggregate accounts for more than 90 per cent of all building material, being mixed with asphalt to pave highways and with Portland cement and sand to make concrete. Dimension (or cut) stone has long been used as the major building block for all types of structures. As a general rule, builders look for what is available locally and make their selection based on such factors as accessibility, end use, climate and so on. For example, certain stones are more resistant to salt corrosion, some have lines of weakness called bedding planes or joints, some are soft and porous, and some are extremely hard and difficult to quarry. On a worldwide basis the five most extensively used building stones are granite, limestone, sandstone, marble and slate.

GRANITE

Granite is a hard, durable, salt-resistant, evenly textured igneous rock that can be polished to a very glossy finish. It can be readily distinguished by its texture, which generally consists of equi-dimensional, tightly interlocking visible crystals

Plate 1.2 Close-up view of granite floor stone, Port Royal.

Table 1.2 X-Ray Fluorescence (XRF) Analysis of Bricks from Various Locations

	Spanish Brickwork, Sevilla Nueva			British Brickwork					Special Brick
% Oxides	Mortar[a]	Seville[b]	Castle site[c]	Colbeck Castle[d]	Spanish Town[e]	Tower Street[f]	Seville[g]	Seville[h]	Fort Clarence[i]
LOM[j]			33.21			0.75		6.87	
Na_2O			0.15			4.59	0.40	0.08	0.64
MgO	1.92	1.41	1.41	2.31	1.89	1.52	1.06	2.22	1.43
Al_2O_3	5.59	11.31	6.10	18.03	20.53	18.14	9.55	14.32	20.68
SiO_2	17.90	23.66	16.11	60.43	60.57	64.52	71.20	55.20	59.54
P_2O_5	0.21	ND*	ND*	0.08	0.31	0.08	0.12	0.13	0.09
SO_3	0.20	0.19	0.09	0.12	0.17	0.13	0.14	0.15	0.13
K_2O	0.62	0.77	0.52	2.09	2.73	2.04	1.94	2.69	2.52
CaO	71.48	57.01	39.44	2.98	3.62	1.46	8.13	10.71	0.94
TiO_2	0.11	0.49	0.32	1.18	1.02	0.64	0.71	0.83	1.06
V_2O_5	ND*	ND*	ND*	0.02	0.03	0.01	0.01	0.01	0.02
Cr_2O_3	0.05	0.01	0.01	0.00	0.00	0.00	0.02	0.02	0.01
MnO	0.04	0.05	0.03	0.19	0.15	0.08	0.07	0.11	0.11
Fe_2O_3	1.30	4.90	2.49	12.25	8.67	5.74	5.35	5.62	11.55
ZnO	0.03	0.02	0.01	0.02	0.02	0.02	0.01	0.01	0.02
SrO	0.12	0.10	0.06	0.04	0.05	0.03	0.02	0.04	0.01
ZrO_2	0.04	0.04	0.02	0.03	0.05	0.03	0.06	0.05	0.03
% Total	99.85	99.85	99.96	99.85	99.85	99.77	98.79	99.06	98.79

[a]White lime mortar on a Spanish brick.
[b]Beige brick with wood fragments from near the Castle site, Seville Park, St Ann.
[c]Pale-brown brick from the Castle site.
[d]Gritty, red-brown brick from Colbeck Castle, St Catherine.
[e]Red brick from Spanish Town Square, St Catherine.
[f]Red brick (with GP initials) made at the General Penitentiary, Kingston.
[g]Orange-brown brick (with RTI initials) imported from the United Kingdom.
[h]Red-brown brick from the old copra-factory chimney at Seville Park, St Ann.
[i]Dark blue-grey engineering brick, Fort Clarence, St Catherine.
[j]Loss of mass, when heated to 1,000°.
*ND=not detected

(grains) of light-coloured minerals, such as quartz, feldspar and muscovite, and dark-coloured minerals, such as hornblende, augite or biotite (Plate 1.2). For further information concerning these terms readers may wish to consult *Minerals and Rocks of Jamaica*.[7] The commonest and perhaps most attractive are the rose-pink and grey varieties. Although granite is difficult to cut, its strength, coupled with its resistance to weathering and its ability to take a long-lasting polish, has made it a favourite for tombstones and wall and floor tiles in many parts of the world. Granite is not known to occur naturally in Jamaica, but its nearest counterpart, granodiorite, outcrops at a few places in the central and eastern sections of the island.

LIMESTONE

Limestone is a moderately hard, sometimes compact, frequently fossil-rich sedimentary rock that can be easily cut and shaped with modern metal tools but can also be fashioned with primitive stone tools that have a greater hardness. Approximately 60 per cent of Jamaica's surface geology is covered by a variable white limestone sequence of rocks, dating back to the beginning of the Eocene epoch (55 million years ago). In 1510 the Spaniards used white limestone in the construction of their first town in Jamaica, Sevilla Nueva. In 1688, when Sir Hans Sloane visited Jamaica, he described the unfinished church at Seville as follows: "Over the place where the Altar was to be, were some Carvings under the ends of the Arches. It was built of a sort of Stone, between Freestone and Marble taken out of a Quarry about a Mile up in the Hills."[8]

In 1937 several carved stones sculpted in high relief were rediscovered by accident and recovered by Charles Cotter.[9] The style of the stones has been described as Renaissance grotesque, and excellent photographs of them have appeared in various publications, notably in a 1938 *West Indian Review* and a 1980 *Jamaica Journal*.[10] It is postulated that they were carved at the town of Sevilla Nueva by a skilled Spanish craftsman who had been brought to the island for that purpose. Geologically speaking, the limestone in the hills behind Seville Great House belongs to the Montpelier Formation, which is a deep-water limestone of Miocene age. It is unfortunate that these beautifully carved stones, instead of being showcased at Seville for all to see, are presently stored at the headquarters of the Institute of Jamaica in Kingston. However, by a stroke of good luck, another opportunity to see such stones *in situ* occurred in 2003 when an archaeological dig, undertaken by Robyn Woodward as part of her PhD programme at Simon Fraser University in Canada, revealed a rich variety of carved objects, including a complete hemispherical font and a large limestone block with an eagle head. If these artefacts could be recovered and displayed, and the nearby quarry from which the stone originated cleaned up and made accessible on foot, Seville Heritage Park would have two additional attractions to offer visitors.

In the late 1960s and early 1970s archaeological excavation work undertaken at Old King's House in Spanish Town uncovered a cellar in which the limestone foundation walls date back to the Spanish period. Majolica ceramic pieces of Spanish origin were also recovered.[11]

Before the advent of cement, bricks and stones were bonded with a mortar composed largely of white lime, made by burning limestone either over an open fire or in stone kilns. The resulting white powder (calcium oxide) was then mixed with earth (often bauxite) or sand and water to make mortar and used in various ways.[12] Lime was also used in the clarification of sugar, but this variety was imported from England.

After the arrival of the British and people of African ancestry, local cut white limestone was used extensively to build bridges, forts, walls, great houses and sugar works (Plate 1.3). Sometimes it was used in conjunction with red brick, a beautiful example of which is the ruins of Colbeck Castle (or House),

Plate 1.3 University Chapel, Mona campus, formerly part of a sugar works in Trelawny, built with Jamaican white limestone.

north of Bodles in St Catherine. But several varieties of imported limestone, notably Portland stone (see chapter 2), Purbeck stone (see chapter 3) and Bath stone (see chapter 4), were used in the construction of certain forts and a few public buildings. Of considerably less importance was Bermuda stone, a very friable, fine-grained limestone used extensively throughout Bermuda for building purposes since the seventeenth century, but which is less durable and more prone to weathering. Although every effort has been made to identify a surviving eighteenth-century structure in Jamaica containing this stone, none has yet been found. But the search continues.

Limestone was also imported for other purposes. For example, in the small cemetery on the Halse Hall estate in Clarendon, there are a few large (up to 7 feet or 2 metres long) dark-grey, fossil-bearing limestone slabs inscribed to the memory of Thomas Hals. On close inspection one can see the skeletal remains of sea urchins (notably parts called ossicles). These gravestones were imported from the United Kingdom, where, geologically speaking, they occur at certain horizons in the Carboniferous Limestone sequence, which is about 350 million years old. This rock was also used in the manufacture of floor tiles, and an excellent example of a black variety, used in combination with white marble, still graces the outside stairway at Richmond Park house, constructed more than two hundred years ago on Half Way Tree Road in Kingston. Here, however, the dominant fossil is a slender spiral-shaped gastropod (*Turritella*) shell.

SANDSTONE

Sandstone is moderately hard, durable and somewhat weather-resistant sedimentary rock that varies in colour from golden-yellow through greenish-grey

Plate 1.4 Flagstone flooring and plinth block made from imported sandstone. Old Naval Hospital, Port Royal.

to reddish-brown. It is composed largely of sand-sized particles of the mineral quartz. In addition to being used as a building stone, sandstone is quite abrasive, and some local varieties were clearly used by the Tainos as whetstones, to shape and polish their stone tools. However, all sandstone slabs (including flagstones) used in the construction of buildings, walls, copings and pavements in Jamaica before 1907 were imported from Yorkshire and elsewhere in England (Plate 1.4).

Also imported were solid, flat circular slabs of natural sandstone, called grindstones or grinding wheels, which, as the name implies, were used for grinding tools and shaping or smoothing other objects or implements. A few are still in use today on various properties throughout the island.

MARBLE

Marble is a fine-grained to coarsely crystalline, essentially non-fossiliferous, metamorphic rock that is composed chiefly of the mineral calcite. The normal colour of pure marble is snow-white, but marble often contains impurities that impart other colours, such as pale blue, grey, green, black, red, maroon and yellow. Certain crystalline limestones that are attractive and can take a polish are commercially marketed as marble, but these are not true marble. Not much is known about the use (if any) of marble during the period of the Spanish occupation (1509–1655), but thereafter it was imported by the British in the form of monuments, tombstones, wall tablets, fonts, floor tiles, table tops and other household items. The elegant 8-foot-tall (about 2.5 metres) statue of Admiral Lord Rodney in the Spanish Town Square was sculpted out of white marble by John Bacon and shipped to Jamaica. The marble, originating in Carrara in the Italian province of Tuscany, was formed by the metamorphism of a Triassic limestone. The statue is housed in an impressive white octagonal temple (see chapter 2). Notable marble monuments are present on the inside walls of the nearby Cathedral Church of St James (also known as the Spanish Town Cathedral), and many of the earliest graves, dating back to the early 1700s, are to be found beneath the flooring. White Italian marble memorial headstones, plaques, monuments and tombstones also exist in many of the older churchyards (cemeteries) – for instance, St Andrew Parish Church (where combinations with granite are also present) and the Jewish Cemetery at Orange Street in downtown Kingston. Black marble from Tournai in Belgium was used to make fonts.

Marble was also imported and used as a floor tile in several Anglican churches, governors' residences and great houses. These square tiles, usually 11 to 12 inches (28 to 30.5 centimetres) on a side, are either creamy white with a very pale bluish tint or dark bluish-grey, sometimes with whitish streaks, and were laid in a checkerboard pattern. Buildings in which this flooring can still be seen include the Cathedral Church in Spanish Town, St Peter's Church at Port Royal (see chapter 3), St James Anglican Church in Montego Bay; Highgate Park House (a former governor's residence) at Sligoville (St Catherine), Seville Great House (St Ann) and Greenwood Great House (St James). The lighter-coloured marble is most likely from Carrara, and so is the blue-grey material, but further microscopic work is necessary to confirm whether England or Ireland might also be a source.

SLATE

Slate is a compact, fine-grained metamorphic rock that possesses a property called slaty cleavage, which permits it to be easily split into slabs and very thin plates (Plate 1.5). As a consequence, it has long been used for roofing shingles (or tiles), for flagstone flooring, to construct buildings and boundary and embankment walls, and as a tablet for writing on with chalk. Most slates are derived from the alteration of shale and are geologically very old. Slate does not occur naturally in Jamaica: it was imported mainly from quarries in Wales, in particular Penrhyn in the Bethesda-Nantlle Belt of northern Gwynedd.

Plate 1.5 Slate on red bricks, Port Royal.

These slates are predominantly purple in colour, and geologically they belong to the Cambrian Period, which makes them about 500 million years old. In 1782, Baron Penrhyn of County Louth inherited the Penrhyn estate and, as noted by Williams, "With money from his family's sugar plantations in Jamaica he created the infrastructure for the largest of all slate quarries which still bears his family name."[13] The roofing slate of St Peter's Church at the Alley in southern Clarendon is largely of this type. Another important reference to Lord Penrhyn is noted in a recent article by Nunes, reporting that Penrhyn's attorney wrote him in 1805 requesting him to send out seventy thousand slate tiles to re-cover a boiling house.[14] The only other slate-roofed buildings still in existence in Jamaica of which I am aware are the small kitchen-restaurant at the Shafston estate Great House in Westmoreland, and sections of the small ancillary buildings on the western (harbour) side of the old Naval Hospital at Port Royal. In 1983, the roofs on two of these buildings were restored using slate tiles from adjoining buildings. And the factory roof at Orange Valley estate in Trelawny used to be covered with purplish slate tiles, but was destroyed in 1988 by hurricane Gilbert.[15]

Another interesting use of slate can be seen on the grounds of the old Naval Hospital. In the perimeter brick wall, on the southeastern side, a layer of slate known as a damp-course is exposed just above the ground surface (Plate 1.1). It was placed at this level to act as a vapour barrier against the upward movement of moisture. Another layer of the same material separates the upper brick course from the overlying limestone copings, but what seems quite unusual is the use of a single vertically placed tile at either end of adjacent copings. The most likely explanation

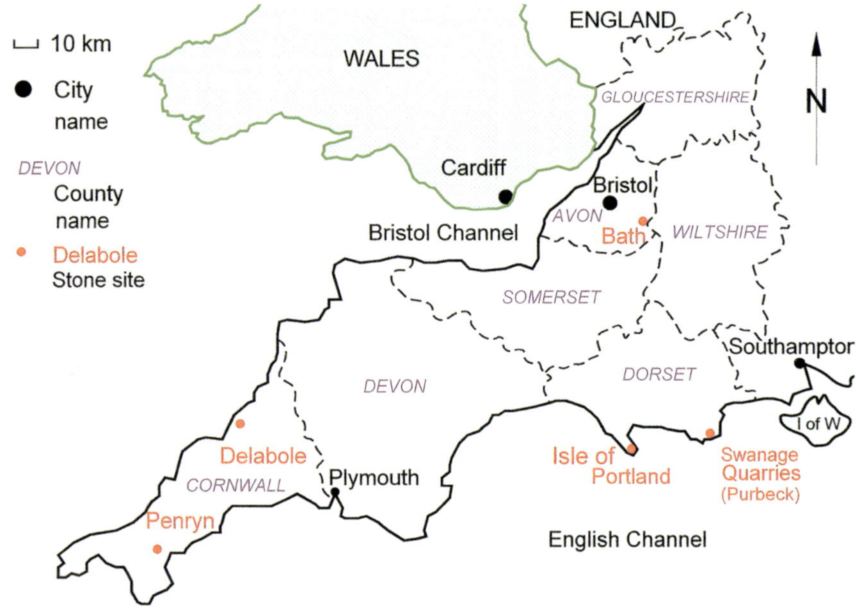

Figure 1.1 Some building stone sites in southwest England.

is that it acts as filler for the joint while adding rigidity to the capping. A layer of damp-proof slate was also placed at ground level in some buildings at Port Royal, the best surviving examples of which are the ancillary buildings at the western and northern ends of the old Naval Hospital. The presence of large (up to 6 feet or 1.8 metres in length), heavy, flat slabs of slate, coloured purple to dark green or blue-grey (sometimes containing small pale-green oval-shaped alteration haloes), should also be noted. It appears that these were used initially to form sloping platforms, called spillways, on which ships were built and repaired. About twenty years ago such slabs could still be found lying around Port Royal, but apparently many have been removed to new "homes" in other parts of Jamaica. Slate has been found elsewhere in the island, but some of the varieties may have originated from the Festiniog Belt in Wales, the Lake District in northern England or the Delabole quarry in Cornwall. Confirmation of this will require detailed mineralogical investigations of the various fragments and slabs, coupled with a review of the quarry and other historical records – a rather daunting task.

The locations in southwest England where some of the major building stones originated are shown in Figure 1.1, and some of the more notable places in Jamaica where they can be seen are listed in Table 1.3.

Table 1.3 Construction Stone Imported between the Late Seventeenth and Mid-Nineteenth Centuries

Rock Class	Rock Type	Colour	Uses	Place found	Place of Origin
Igneous	Granite	Light grey	Floorstone	Old Naval Hospital, Port Royal	Cornwall (probably near Penryn), England
		Light grey	Copestone	St John's Church, Black River, St Elizabeth	Cornwall, Devon or Cumberland, England
Sedimentary	Sandstone	Tan to yellow-brown	Copestone	Old Naval Hospital	Yorkshire, England
		Shades of red; pale green to yellow-green, purple and brown	Flagstone, paving stone, floorstone	Fortifications, plantations, great houses, early government offices	Yorkshire and other counties in England
	Limestone	Buff to grey-brown	Floorstone	Fort Charles, Port Royal	Purbeck, Dorset county, South England
		Buff to grey-brown	Paving stone, walling	Fort Augusta, St Catherine	Purbeck, Dorset county, south England
		Pale grey	Paving stone, walling	Fort Augusta, St Catherine	England

Table 1.3 continues

Table 1.3 continued

Sedimentary *(continued)*	Limestone *(continued)*	White to pale buff	Parapet wall	Fort Augusta, St Catherine	Bath, England
		White to pale buff	Columns	Old King's House, Spanish Town, St Catherine	Isle of Portland, England
		White, weathering to a light tan-brown	Floorstone, column	Good Hope, Trelawny	Suspected to be from the Isle of Portland, England
		White	Walling	Not yet substantiated	Bermuda
		Dark grey to black	Tombstones, floorstone	Various cemeteries, churchyards and churches	England
Metamorphic	Slate	Dark grey	Tombstones, floorstone	Various cemeteries, churchyards and churches	Wales or England (possibly from Delabole in Cornwall)
		Purple or green	Roofing	St Peter's Church (Alley); Port Royal; some estates	Penrhyn, Wales
		Dark spinach-green with tiny pyrite cubes	Roofing	Good Hope and other estates in Trelawny	Wales or Scotland (possibly Argyll county)
	Marble	White	Monuments, wall plaques, flooring, tombstones	Island-wide	Carrara and Massa, in Tuscany province, Italy
		Dark blue to grey	Flooring	Some churches, great houses and other buildings	Probably mainland Europe

OTHER STONE TYPES

In addition to the stones described above, other naturally occurring lithic material was brought to the island for purposes other than construction (Table 1.4). These materials are described in more detail below.

Table 1.4 Other Imported Stone Types and Country of Origin

Name	Colour	Notable Features	Uses	Place of Origin
Flint	Dark-grey to black	Texture, hardness, conchoidal fracture	Gunflints	Brandon, on border of Norfolk and Suffolk counties, SE England
	Honey-amber	Colour and hardness	Gunflints	France
Limestone	White	Fine-grained, very porous	Filtering stone, dripstone	Barbados
Calcareous sandstone	Buff to pale grey	Salt-and-pepper-like appearance	Filtering stone, dripstone	Reportedly Tenerife, Canary Islands
Sandstone	Pale yellow-brown	Fine-grained and gritty	Grindstones	Derbyshire, England
Jade or jadeitite	Green	Smoothly ground objects, tough, hard and compact	Utilitarian or ceremonial	Unknown; possibly Guatemala
Gneiss	Reddish-brown	Smoothly ground; minerals in roughly parallel bands	Utilitarian or ceremonial	Unknown; possibly Hispaniola or the eastern Caribbean
Assorted igneous and metamorphics	Generally dark	Variable, but some contain crystals of green olivine	Ballast for sailing ships	Various locations throughout England

CHERT AND FLINT

Chert is a hard (H=7), dense microcrystalline sedimentary rock, composed of very tightly interlocking crystals of quartz (less than 30 microns in diameter), but amorphous silica (or poor opal) may also be present. Chert exhibits a conchoidal fracture and varies in colour from white through pale grey to brown. Although flint is chemically the same, this term is usually applied to the very dark-grey to black varieties. Chert occurs mainly as rounded to elliptically shaped nodules in limestone and dolomite and, less commonly, as layered deposits (bedded chert) and narrow lenses.

In Jamaica, chert occurs principally in a chalky limestone called the Montpelier Formation, which outcrops mainly in a narrow band along the north side of the island, and close to the coast in eastern St Andrew and St Thomas. One of the best examples of its use as a building material is found in the walls at Seville Heritage Park, located just west of the town of St Ann's Bay. Weathering of the limestone in this area liberated these large nodular cherts (locally called flintstone) and subsequent transportation by running water left them scattered about on the surface of the land, where they were easily gathered and set in mortar. One of the notable features of the walls is the absence of horizontal layers; instead they are uncoursed fieldstone, composed mainly of chert with some limestone and marble fragments. Another physical property of chert (and flint) is its ability to fracture and produce razor-sharp edges. As a consequence, flint was used as both a tool and weapon by prehistoric civilizations. In Jamaica it appears that the Tainos used it as a scraping tool (hence the term *scrapers*) and as a cutting tool. Chert or flint fragments are found in most Taino occupation sites, indicating that they were transported or traded by the Tainos. Centuries later, the British imported another variety of flint for use in muskets and pistols (see chapter 7).

VOLCANIC ROCKS

Volcanic (or extrusive) rocks form when hot molten matter, called magma, is extruded, or forced out, onto the Earth's surface. Exposure to the much cooler surface temperatures causes the molten mass to chill and harden rapidly. The resulting rocks may be either glassy or very fine-grained, or they may contain larger, well-formed lath-shaped crystals, called phenocrysts, set in a finely crystalline matrix called the groundmass. Examples range from light-coloured keratophyres, dacites and felsites to dark-coloured andesites and basalts. The presence in Jamaica of a wide variety of these volcanic rocks (especially in the eastern and central parts of the island) is well known and documented.[16] And many of the stone implements used by the Tainos for utilitarian, religious and ceremonial purposes were derived from this group of rocks. So, too, was much of the river sand and gravel that have been used since 1655 for construction purposes.

GREENSTONE

Another type of rock that was used by the Tainos is greenstone. This is an umbrella name applied to very fine-grained, green-coloured, hard, nonfoliated metamorphic rocks that are difficult to accurately classify without resorting to destructive methods of analysis. Some of the smoothly ground, highly polished petaloid celts fashioned by the Tainos are difficult to identify, as the original texture is no longer visible. To identify them with certainty, it is necessary to cut very thin slices and examine them under a polarizing microscope. Clearly this is not the preferred option, especially if the specimen is museum-perfect. To illustrate the point, in describing the material from which the celts are made, Duerden stated, "Dolerite is rather common as well as a greenish schist, and others graduating between quartzites and gneisses. A metamorphic siliceous green rock resembling jade, and taking a high polish, is met with. Most of the material is such as occurs in the island."[17] Was this a greenstone or true jade? In 1975, Roobol and Lee reported that of some 450 celts found in Jamaica, 78 per cent were composed of "greenstone"; the term, as they used it, included nephrite, which is the more common variety of jade. They did point out, however, that up to that time jade had not been identified in Jamaica.[18] Although no naturally occurring jade has yet been discovered in the island, a recent study of a petaloid celt found in the parish of Manchester has confirmed that it is composed largely of jadeite (see chapter 5).

BALLAST STONES

It is well known that several centuries ago, sailors used heavy substances in the holds of sailing vessels to improve their stability and maintain the desired draft or trim. Such substances were referred to as ballast and included boulders, bricks, slabs of sandstone, slate, granite and the like. Boulders and pebbles of very old igneous rocks, such as olivine basalt, and metamorphic rocks, such as schists and gneisses, that were brought to the island as ballast in ships can still be found along some shorelines (for example, Palisadoes) and in some harbours (in particular Annotto Bay and Falmouth). These were offloaded to make room for the returning cargo, which was chiefly sugar. According to the records, several bills were presented to the House of Assembly to regulate the mooring of ships to restrain "all masters or commanders of vessels, for the future, from heaving overboard ballast".[19] But many of the building materials that can still be seen today – bricks and flagstone, for instance – initially served as ballast on the outward journey from England and elsewhere.

2

Built Heritage

When the British forces invaded Jamaica and captured it from the Spaniards in 1655, the island was underdeveloped. In the 1700s, however, the production and export of sugar rapidly transformed it into one of the most prosperous small islands in the world. One of the legacies of this period is the large number of built structures that sprang up all over the island, notably aqueducts, bridges, chimneystacks, churches, fortifications, great houses, kilns, public buildings, sugar factories, tower mills and walls. Such structures – the result of intense manual labour – have played a vital role in the history of Jamaica. The choice of material used in their construction depended on the local availability of suitable building stone. Consequently, many are built of white limestone, which is abundant throughout much of the island. But large quantities of burnt red brick were also brought from England. It served as ballast stone on the outward voyage, and then on arrival in Jamaica was offloaded and used in the construction of many structures, often in combination with cut white limestone blocks and lime mortar.

In the nineteenth century, red brick (both imported and local varieties) and white limestone continued to be the most important building materials used in Jamaica. But the large-scale production and availability of cheaper yellow-brown stock bricks near London, England, led to their importation and use in the construction of walls, churches and other structures. Other stones were also shipped out from England, Scotland and Wales and used in the construction of many buildings. Fortunately, despite the ravages of hurricanes, earthquakes, weathering and man, many of these survive and continue to serve a useful purpose to this day.

Table 2.1 Comparison of Various Brick Dimensions

Location of Bricks	Maker's Stamp	Length inches (cm)	Width inches (cm)	Thickness inches (cm)	Notable Features
Kingston (Tower Street)[a]	G.P.	9.0 (23)	4.50 (11.5)	2.87 (7.3)	Brick-red with many pea-sized fragments
Port Royal (old Naval Hospital)[a]	G.P.H.K.	9.0 (23)	4.25 (10.8)	2.70 (6.6)	
Port Royal (Fort Charles)	None	9.0 (23)	4.12 (10.5)	2.12 (5.4)	Brick-red; sandy texture
Port Royal (sunken city)[b]	None	9.0 (23)	4.25 (10.8)	2.25 (5.7)	Greyish; fine-grained
St Catherine (Guanaboa Vale)	None	9.2 (23.5)	4.62 (11.8)	3.25 (8.2)	Dark red; sandy texture
St Catherine (Colbeck Castle)	None	8.5 (21.6)	4.25 (10.8)	2.50 (6.5)	Dark red; sandy texture
St Ann (Seville Heritage Park)[c]	RTI	9.0 (23)	4.20 (10.5)	2.50 (6.5)	Yellow-brown with small black flecks
Trelawny (Falmouth)[c]	RTI	9.0 (23)	4.25 (10.8)	2.62 (6.6)	
St Ann (Castle site, Seville)[d]	None	12.0 (30.4)	5.75 (14.7)	2.00 (5.1)	Tan; with wood & shells
St Ann (Castle site, Seville)[e]	None	9.0 (23)	3.75 (9.6)	1.50 (3.8)	Red; smooth sides
Clarendon (Vere)	IMG VERE	9.25 (23.5)	4.37 (11.1)	3.25 (8.2)	Orange-red; sandy texture
Trelawny	PEZ	9.0 (23)	4.25 (10.8)	2.25 (5.7)	Pale grey-brown
St Catherine (Fort Clarence)	Star of David	8.5 (21.6)	4.19 (10.7)	2.81 (7.1)	Dark grey and heavy

[a]Made by inmates of the General Penitentiary in either Kingston or Spanish Town.
[b]Retrieved about 100 metres offshore (between the old Naval Hospital and the Fort James buoy).
[c]Imported London stock brick.
[d]Manufactured by the Spanish at Seville.
[e]Probably imported.

BRICK AND LIMESTONE CONSTRUCTION

As noted in the previous chapter, a brick is a rectangular building block made from clay. Initially all bricks were made by drying hand-shaped blocks of mud in the sun. Later they were shaped in moulds and placed in large ovens, called kilns, and heated (baked or fired) to very high temperatures. Typically, most bricks are red or reddish-brown in colour owing to the presence of iron oxide, but other shades and hues can be obtained either by incorporating other substances (such as chalk and ash) or by varying the firing. Although there are literally hundreds of types of bricks to suit different purposes, they can be divided into two general groups: building bricks and refractory bricks. A standard building brick consists of six sides: two faces (called stretchers), two ends (called headers), and a top and bottom (called the bed), which correspond respectively to length, thickness, and width. Typical building bricks range from 8 to 9 inches (20 to 22 centimetres) in length, 3.5 to 4.5 inches (9 to 11 centimetres) in width, and 2 to 3 inches (5 to 7.5 centimetres) in height, but the actual dimensions of a few from various sites throughout the island are shown in Table 2.1.

Refractory bricks are special heat-resistant bricks of variable size, used chiefly to line furnaces.

The manner in which bricks are arranged and laid down is a vital component in forming a stable structure. To achieve stability they are placed in horizontal layers, called courses, and laid in patterns, called bonds, in which either their short ends (headers) or long ends (stretchers) are exposed on the face of the wall (see Figure 2.1). As expected, there are many types of arrangements, but one of the strongest and most popular of all patterns is the Flemish bond, which consists of a series of alternating headers and stretchers within each course. Other common bond arrangements used in construction include English bond (alternating courses of headers and stretchers), American bond (one row of headers to four of stretchers), Scottish bond (one row of headers to five of stretchers), header bond (composed entirely of headers) and running bond (composed entirely of stretchers). Additional features included in some structures are 1) courses of bricks laid with their long sides upright, called a Soldier bond; 2) random mixtures of headers and stretchers, called a Wild bond; 3) a long horizontal layer, called a string course, composed of another type of material; and 4) non-rectangular bricks, called "Specials", which are made in various shapes for special purposes.

Bricklaying is not as simple as it looks; it is, in fact, a skilled trade that takes many years to perfect. In the eighteenth and nineteenth centuries the manufacture of bricks in Britain had improved tremendously compared with earlier periods, when the crudely made bricks were irregular in both shape and size. But better blending and moulding of various types of clay, combined with higher firing temperatures, led to greater consistency. Bricks were available in a wide variety of colours, of which red was the most fashionable up to 1730. Patterned effects, however, were achieved by strategically placing dark-coloured overcooked headers, ranging from

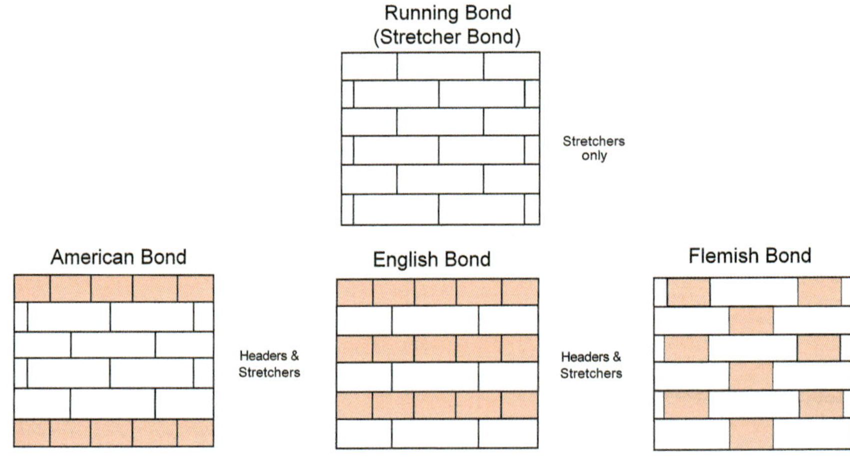

Figure 2.1 Arrangement and comparison of the common bond types.

Plate 2.1 London stock bricks and Jamaican limestone quoins. St John's Anglican Church, Black River.

deep purple to dark slate-grey or black, throughout the walling.

During the Victorian period in England (1837–1901), most bricks were machine-made. They can be recognized by their smooth surface, large size and sharp outline. Production of bricks from yellow-brown marl clay, near London, England, commenced on a grand scale. Two types – a bright yellow and a yellow-brown with black flecks – known as London stock bricks were manufactured, and thousands of them were shipped to Jamaica (Plate 2.1). A yellow-grey variety from Cambridgeshire, known as Gault bricks, may also have been shipped to the island. In addition to size, shape and colour, another important feature of bricks is the texture. Some are uniformly fine-grained, while others have a gritty exterior, often as a result of sand being sprinkled into the mould to prevent the clay from sticking to it during firing. The least attractive are the very coarse-grained variety with the clearly visible remains of large pebble-sized fragments, the identification of which may be an important clue in ascertaining the source of the clay. Unfortunately, many fine brickwork structures throughout Jamaica have been damaged by earthquakes and hurricanes, but evidence of the craftsmanship of eighteenth- and nineteenth-century brickmakers and bricklayers is still to be found in many places throughout the island.

In addition to bricks, there are all sorts of rocks that can be used to build walls and other structures, including limestone, sandstone, granite, marble and slate. In Jamaica the most important of these is limestone, a naturally formed sedimentary rock composed essentially of the mineral calcite. It is deposited in layers or beds ranging in thickness from a centimetre to a metre or two, which are distinguishable from the layers above and below. The junction between layers, however, is invariably quite weak, and where they are parallel it is often possible to extract slabs of uniformly thick limestone.

Approximately 60 per cent of Jamaica's surface area is covered by white limestone, in varying degrees of compactness, toughness, permeability, porosity, age and fossil content, collectively called the White Limestone Group. In general, the limestone formations that comprise this group are either soft and friable or moderately hard and compact; in either case, Jamaican white limestone can be cut with a saw blade or shaped with a hammer and metal file. Planes of weakness or breakage, called joints, are common everywhere in the bedrock, and this frequently allows for the easy removal of material. A not-too-common feature is the presence within the limestone of rounded, pebble- to boulder-sized nodules of comparatively very hard flint or chert. Over the last several million years, weathering and erosion has aided in their liberation, and in some places a carpet of loose material can be seen. Flint and chert are too hard and splintery to be dressed and shaped with ordinary metal tools, but because of their toughness and resistance to abrasion, walls made of this material can survive for centuries.

WALLS

In many ancient centres of civilization, walls were constructed of irregular blocks of roughly trimmed stone, either stacked loosely on top of one another without any cementing material or mortar or wedged carefully together with the intervening spaces filled with smaller fragments of stone and clay. In regions where surface stone was not available, local clay was used to make sun-dried bricks. It was subsequently discovered that lime mixed with water, with or without sand, could be used to bond bricks and stone. The addition of volcanic ash to this mix by the Romans, more than two thousand years ago, led to the invention of concrete. This material was considerably harder and stronger and greatly facilitated the development of the arch by the Romans.

During the Middle Ages (AD 400–1500), natural stone and man-made bricks remained the choice materials for masonry purposes throughout Europe and elsewhere. And plaster made from lime, usually with the addition of coarse sand, was used to finish the panels between the timbers of wooden-framed buildings. The use of lime mortar continued until the mid-1820s when Joseph Aspidin, a British bricklayer, invented Portland cement, a fine grey powder that hardens when mixed with water. After the 1907 earthquake, building construction in Jamaica underwent another major transformation with the introduction of reinforced concrete, steel and prefabricated panels.

Like brick, walls constructed of stone laid down in horizontal layers are described as coursed. If the stones are rectangular or square and roughly the same height, the masonry is referred to as "coursed ashlar", and where the masonry is composed of roughly shaped stones that fit on approximately level beds or layers, the term "coursed rubble" is applied. By contrast, walls built of a jumbled mass of stone (sometimes with broken bricks) are said to be uncoursed. While hiking the countryside in search of walls constructed before and at the beginning of the twentieth century, I observed the following main types of walls.

COURSED WALLS

Coursed walls were preferred where elegance, architectural symmetry and foundation stability were desired and could be afforded (Plate 2.2). As a consequence, many of the finest surviving structures on the island, built by various governments, rich landowners, merchants and others, fall into this group. These were constructed from bricks only, from white limestone blocks only (squared or rectangular), from combinations of brick and limestone, and from other stone types.

Plate 2.2 Boundary wall built with bauxite, lime and cut white slimestone blocks. Wigton property, Manchester.

UNCOURSED WALLS

Less costly and elaborate walls that served mainly to divide and enclose are of several types.

• Dry stack or dry stone walls were the main type of field boundary in early Jamaica. These walls were composed largely of roughly trimmed pieces of white limestone or other rock types that were fitted and then tightly packed together, without cement, to keep them in place.

• Wet stack rubble stone walls were composed of various stones bonded by a cementing agent, most commonly a mix of lime and bauxite, lime and clay, or lime and earth. The walls were composed largely of limestone, a mix of other rock types, or flint or chert, or a combination.

• Wattle and daub construction consists of bamboo poles or wooden sticks (wattle) woven together in a lattice-like pattern and plastered with lime and earth (daub).

• A "nog" or "Spanish wall" was built with timber, burnt lime and various types of stone. Hardwood frames are held together by wooden crossbars, and the intervening spaces are in-filled with stone and lime mortar.

ARCHES, BRIDGES AND AQUEDUCTS

An arch is a curved structure that spans open space and can support overlying weight. It was developed by the Romans around 300 BC and, to this day, remains one of the most important construction forms ever conceived. Before arches, builders had to place stone columns (piers) close together to support the weight of stone slabs, because the material had a tendency to break under its own weight when the piers were widely separated.

In its simplest form, a brick or stone arch consists of wedge-shaped blocks called *voussoirs,* or archstones, which rest on springers. During construction a wooden frame is usually placed below the blocks to provide support until the last wedge-shaped stone, called the keystone, is inserted in the centre at the top of the arch (see Figure 2.2 and Plate 2.3). When the frame is removed, compression from both sides against the keystone keeps the arch in place. By avoiding tension entirely in their arches, the Romans discovered a most important construction principle, and succeeded in building a huge network of artificial channels, called aqueducts, to supply the city of Rome with water. Bridges with semicircular arches were also constructed to span obstacles, such as rivers.

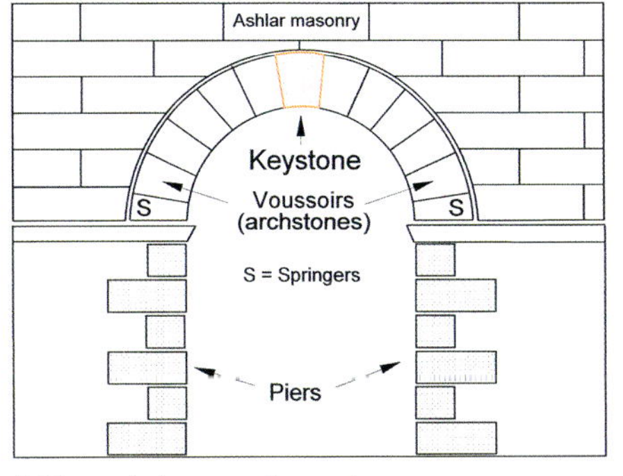

(A) The main features of an arch

(B) Quoin stones (Q) set in a coursed brick wall

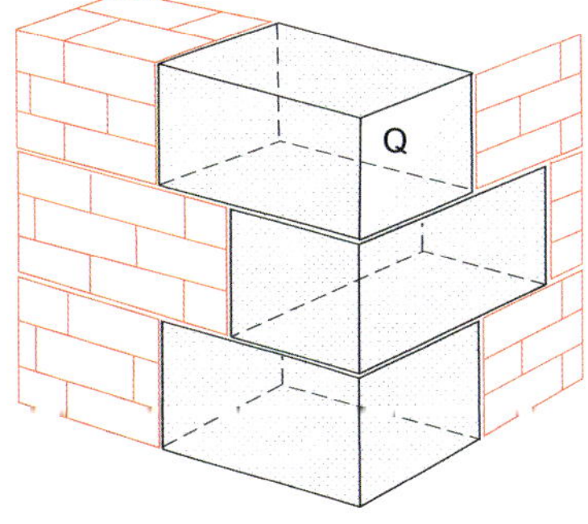

Figure 2.2 Illustration of some building terms.

Plate 2.3 Brick arch with keystone dated 1759. Mona campus, University of the West Indies.

In Jamaica, many aqueducts were built on sugar estates to irrigate crops and also to supply the refineries with water. One of the first and best preserved is the Hope Aqueduct, near Papine, which was completed in 1758 and remains in good condition. Further south, on the Mona campus of the University of the West Indies, are the interesting remains of the old sugar works, constructed out of brick and a wide variety of stone types from the banks and bed of the nearby Hope River.[1] For more information on its history, see *Mona, Past and Present*.[2]

In 1845 rail service commenced with the completion of a line between Kingston and Angels (just north of Spanish Town). This was followed by an extension to Old Harbour, and between 1882 and 1885 rail lines were extended from Old Harbour to Porus and from Angels to Ewarton via Bog Walk. In 1894, rail transportation between western and eastern sections of the island was finally realized with the completion of the line from Porus to Montego Bay via Catadupa. During the same period, a network of roads developed in conjunction with the construction of several stone bridges, which permitted access to many parts of the interior. The use of dynamite, invented by Alfred Nobel in 1867, contributed greatly to the success of the transportation infrastructure, as much rock had to be blasted, especially for the construction of several railway tunnels.

CHIMNEYS, LIME KILNS AND TOWER MILLS

The passage through which smoke is led away from a fireplace, furnace or oven is called a chimney. The characteristic form on eighteenth- and nineteenth-century sugar plantations throughout Jamaica was a tall, narrow, free-standing vertical shaft, either square or rectangular in cross-section and tapering uniformly towards the top. Chimneys were made with brick or limestone or a combination.

Lime was manufactured by burning limestone in chambers called kilns, which were themselves constructed of limestone but were lined on the inside with bricks to prevent conversion of the limestone to white lime every time the kiln was fired. Of the few that still exist, one is box-like in shape with openings on all sides, and the rest resemble truncated beehives.

Plate 2.4 St John's Anglican Church, Black River.

Another abandoned legacy from the colonial past, many examples of which are still well preserved, is a structure called a tower mill. This was part of a device built to harness energy from the wind for grinding sugar cane. It consisted of two outwardly visible parts: a stationary beehive-like body built out of cut white limestone, and a movable cap with vanes, or sails, which would spin when facing the wind – hence the name windmill. It has been reported that in 1804 there were about ninety mills in operation, but today very little remains of the system of vanes and gears that played a vital role in the development of Jamaica's sugar industry.[3]

Plate 2.5 The magnificent Anglican Christchurch at Port Antonio, built in 1840. Tall, narrow, round-arch windows up to 18 feet (6 metres) in height are a distinctive feature of this brick and limestone building.

CHURCHES

One of the most visible legacies of the island under British rule is the many solidly built churches that are to be found throughout every parish in Jamaica. Initially they were constructed of imported or local red bricks or local white limestone. In the nineteenth century several were built out of the yellow-brown stock bricks from London, two beautiful examples of which are St Thomas Anglican Church at Bluefields, in the parish of Westmoreland, and St John's Parish Church in the town of Black River, St Elizabeth (Plate 2.4). But perhaps the finest and architecturally most elegant brick-and-limestone church, with its distinctive tall, narrow window frames with rounded arches at the top, is Christchurch in Port Antonio (Plate 2.5).

FORTS AND BARRACKS

After taking Jamaica from the Spanish in 1655, the British quickly set about erecting coastal fortifications, initially at Port Royal to guard the entrance to Kingston Harbour. Only a badly shaken Fort Charles remained standing after the great earthquake of 1692. Two years later, Rock Fort at the eastern end of the harbour was fortified, and by 1699 the reconstruction of Fort Charles was complete. During the eighteenth century, permanent defences were built at several other strategic coastal sites around the island – notably Fort Augusta at Mosquito Point in Kingston Harbour (see chapter 4), Fort Lindsay at Port Morant, Fort George at Port Antonio, Fort Brunswick at Annotto Bay, Fort Haldane at Port Maria, Fort Dundas at Rio Bueno, Fort Balcarres at Falmouth, Fort Frederick at Montego Bay, Fort Charlotte at Lucea, and Fort Carlisle, near the mouth of Rio Minho in Clarendon.

PUBLIC BUILDINGS AND MONUMENTS

The unearthed remains of a fort, house and old sugar works at New Seville (Sevilla Nueva), on the western side of St Ann's Bay, are the only known structures of unquestionable Spanish origin that can still be seen today. In 1534, the Spaniards ceased occupation of this site and transferred their capital to present-day Spanish Town, which they called Villa de la Vega, the Town in the Plain. It remained the Spanish capital for over a century and the British capital for more than two, but apart from the town's basic layout there is no above-ground trace of a Spanish presence. Under British rule, Spanish Town became the administrative, ecumenical and social centre of the island, but in 1872 the capital was formally transferred to Kingston.

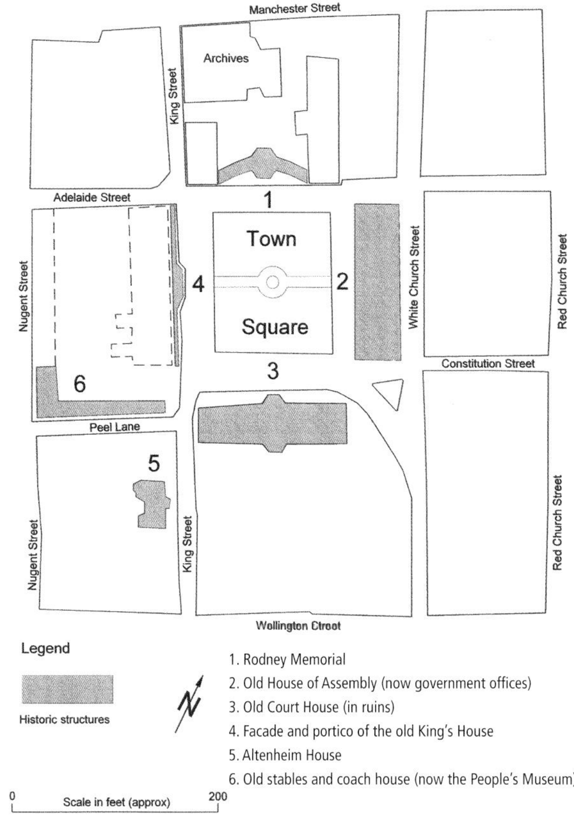

Figure 2.3 Spanish Town Square historic structures.

For those who are attracted to buildings and other structures of historic and architectural significance, the former capital of Jamaica, Spanish Town, still has much to offer, despite the ravages of hurricanes, earthquakes and fires, and decades of human neglect. But it is the Spanish Town Square and its environs, in the centre of the town, that take us back to an era when tradesmen and builders were masters in the art of building with brick. In the very heart of the town are the remains of the best collection of historic buildings in the island. These, described below, are centred in the old square, or parade, as it was originally called (see Figure 2.3), and adjoining areas.

The memorial to Admiral Lord Rodney is on the north side. It includes a large statue, carved out of white Carrara marble by the well-known English sculptor John Bacon. Because of its colour and homogeneous nature, this particular marble has long been prized for sculptures. Behind the memorial are the Jamaica Archives, built in 1962, and the Island Records Office, which is the home of numerous important historical documents, including deeds, patents, wills, court records, church records and plantation journals, dating back to the seventeenth century.

Plate 2.6 Portico columns made from British Portland stone. Old King's House, Spanish Town.

On the east side is the oldest House of Assembly building, still very impressive with its exquisite architectural design. Constructed of red bricks and sandstone flags in the early 1760s, it has over the years undergone some alteration and remedial restoration. Today, the building is occupied by local government offices of the St Catherine Parish Council.

On the south side is a red-brick late Georgian building, the construction of which was not completed until the early 1800s (about 1818). Known as the Court House, this once beautiful structure – which withstood the onslaught of many hurricanes and a powerful earthquake in 1907 – was tragically gutted by fire in 1986, leaving only the walls and the charred remains of a few wooden beams, precariously perched at ceiling height. For safety reasons, the whole area has been fenced off.

Occupying the west side of the square is the old Georgian King's House, with its adjoining stables and coach house. Built in 1765, it served as the official residence for all the governors of Jamaica until 1872. Describing the building as he saw it in 1773, the noted historian Edward Long wrote:

> The first floor is raised about four feet above the ground; the second is an Attic story; the length of the façade is about two hundred feet; and of the whole range, including the yard and offices, about two hundred and sixty. The cornices, key-stones, pediments, copings, and quoins, are of beautiful free-stone, dug out of the Hope river course, in St Andrew's parish. The entrance is by a lofty portico, projecting from the middle of the front about fifteen feet, supported by twelve columns of Portland-stone, of the Ionic order. . . . The pavement of the portico is of white marble, the ascent to which is by a flight of steps of the same material.[4]

Unfortunately, on the night of Friday, 9 October 1925, a fire of unknown origin swept through the main building, doing extensive damage,[5] and all that remains today is the eastern brick-walled façade with limestone quoins, the large columns described by Long (each consisting of a base, un-fluted shaft and Ionic capital made of Portland stone) and white marble steps (Plate 2.6). Geologically speaking, Portland stone is a naturally occurring, fine-grained limestone with an oolitic texture (reminiscent of fish roe; see glossary) that was deposited about 150 million years ago, during the Jurassic period. It is obtained from quarries on the Isle of Portland in the county of Dorset on the south coast of England. Following the Great Fire of London in 1666, boatload after boatload of huge blocks of Portland stone was carried along the south coast and up the river Thames and used in the construction of many famous buildings, most notably St Paul's Cathedral, Sir Christopher Wren's architectural masterpiece. The oolitic texture is not easily discernible on the tall shafts in Spanish Town, owing to the many coats of whitewash and paint that have been applied over the years. However, around the base where the paint has flaked off or small chips have broken away, it is still possible to make it out with the aid of a magnifying glass.

Plate 2.7 A wall-mounted Barbados dripstone Altenheim House, Spanish Town.

In the early 1960s, the old stables and coach house that survived the fire were converted into a Folk Museum, the name of which has since been changed to the People's Museum.

The streets around the square still contain a number of Georgian-style houses with jalousie-shuttered windows, fretwork verandahs, various staircase designs and brick walls, and marble-covered front steps. Another interesting feature is the incorporation of dripstones (also called filtering stones, for purifying drinking water) into some walls; perhaps the best surviving example is the one built into a vertical recess under the staircase at the back of Altenheim House on King Street (Plate 2.7). Unfortunately, this historic structure – presently owned by the Institute of Jamaica – is badly run down and in urgent need of repair if it is to be saved.

Situated about 900 feet (275 metres) to the southeast of the square is the cathedral, affectionately referred to by many as the Spanish Town Cathedral. It stands on the site of the Spanish Chapel of the Red Cross, which was destroyed by British soldiers at the time of the invasion. In the early 1700s an Anglican church was built on the site, but it was destroyed by a hurricane in 1712. According to the memorial tablet over the main door at the west, the present red-brick structure was rebuilt upon its old foundation in 1714. Later additions and alterations include the tower with the white cupola in 1831 and the perpendicular-style chancel with side aisles in 1848–49. It was originally called the parish church of St Catherine, but in 1843 it became the Cathedral of the Jamaica Diocese. Inside the church are many elaborate marble monuments and wall tablets, and there are gravestones in the transept aisle. Outside the south door, on the pavement, are several very heavy dark-grey gravestones of imported limestone, some as large as 6 feet by 3 feet, and on the wall above are ornamental carvings of faces with African features. In the churchyard are several tombs made of brick, imported limestone and marble, and other materials.

3

Port Royal: Its Geologic Heritage

June 7, 1692 – This day happened the great earthquake which destroyed Port Royal, and did great injury throughout the island: The council had previously met in that town, and it is probable were sitting when it commenced, as no adjournment is entered that day in their journal.[1]

Port Royal is arguably the most famous town in all the Caribbean. It is located at the western end of a narrow 9-mile-long (almost 14 kilometres) sand and gravel spit, known as the Palisadoes, that serves as a natural breakwater for Kingston Harbour. My fascination with the town dates back some fifty or more years to when I was a small boy, listening intently to tales about its riotous and romantic past and its devastation by the great earthquake of 1692. The image was enhanced by the spectacle, in the early 1950s, of a few tilted buildings projecting out a short distance into Kingston Harbour, a stark reminder of the effects of another severe earthquake in 1907. Although those buildings have since collapsed, I have remained magnetically attracted – so much so that, notwithstanding the earlier excavations of Edwin Link (1959), Robert Marx (1966–68), Phillip Mayes (1969–70), Anthony Priddy (1971–74) and Professor Hamilton of Texas A&M (1981–90), I have been trying to find answers to some puzzling questions that those investigations did not address.

As many readers know, the history of Port Royal – once described as the richest and wickedest city in the Western Hemisphere – has been the subject of numerous books, television documentaries, journal papers and newspaper articles.[2] But not much has been written about the materials used in the construction of the town. In some institutions of higher learning this field of study comes under "industrial archaeology" but, because Port Royal is unique, the subject might also be included in "heritage geology" or "geo-heritage studies". No matter what you choose to call it, the full story of Port Royal's built history has not yet been told. The question is, why? I would venture to say that over the years Port Royal has been studied largely by historians, naval explorers, and marine and terrestrial archaeologists, with little input from earth scientists or geologists.

GEOLOGIC SETTING

A spit is a finger-like expanse of land, composed of sand or gravel, that extends from the shore into a body of water. Geologically speaking, the origin of the Palisadoes spit is quite complex, but research suggests that it goes back to a time during the Pleistocene epoch when sea level was some 130 feet (40 metres) lower than today.[3] Before that, huge volumes of rock were eroded by the Hope River and other streams and laid down in fan-shaped deposits at the foot of the mountains, giving rise to what are known today as the Liguanea Plains. Then, near the end of the Pliocene epoch, about 2.5 to 2 million years ago, changes in geological conditions resulted in a diversion of the Hope River to its present course past August Town to Harbour View. With this shift, a new delta was formed at Harbour View, and many of the smaller silt-, sand- and gravel-sized fragments were carried out into the sea, where they were transported in a westerly direction by currents and wave action (Figure 3.1). Thus, the present Palisadoes spit is the product of a long

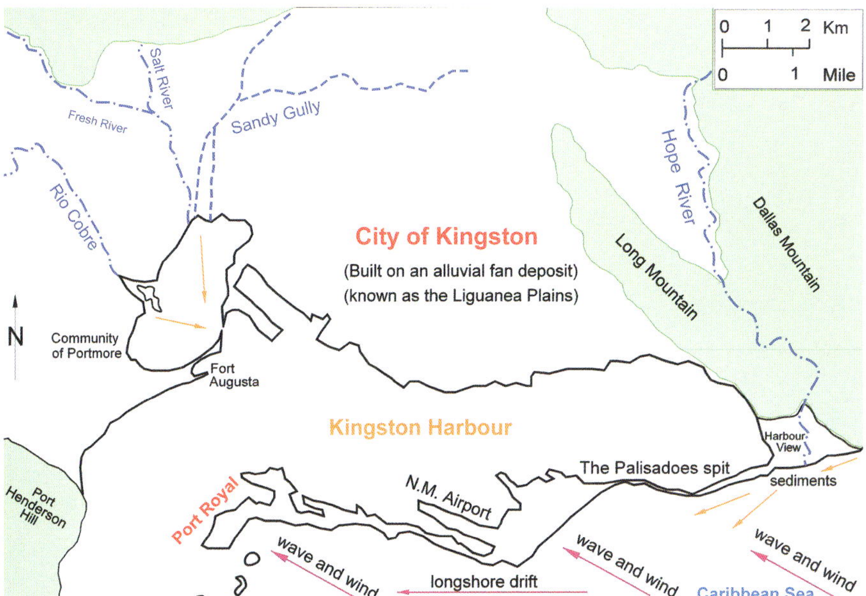

Figure 3.1 Major physical features and processes in the Kingston area.

period of erosion followed by deposition of primarily sand and gravel on the surface of a number of former banks, cays and coral reefs. As it grew westward, incorporating several other pre-existing islands, it acted to some extent as a barrier to the silt brought down by the Rio Cobre, Fresh River and gullies draining the Liguanea Plains.

In 1655, when the British captured Jamaica from the Spanish, Port Royal was an island, which they referred to as Cagway Point or Point-Cagua.[4] Sometime between October 1663 and October 1664 the name Port Royal appears in the records.[5] Port Royal would remain an island for many years, until deposition of sand and gravel connected it to the rest of the Palisadoes spit. In 1960, a borehole sunk at Port Royal passed through gravel, sand and silt deposits before encountering coralline limestone at 140 feet (about 43 metres), thereby proving that the town was built on poorly consolidated sediments. Notwithstanding the absence of clay and outcrops of rock, there is no other place of comparable size in Jamaica where one can find the diversity of building stones such as exists at Port Royal. For in addition to the three major classes of rocks – igneous, sedimentary and metamorphic – there is a variety of man-made bricks and mortar.

This mix of material in such a small area has long amazed and fascinated visitors to Port Royal, both local and from overseas, who often ask, "Where did all these stones come from?" Except for the sand and gravel, every other building material has been imported – including the lime and white limestone blocks – but from where? Initially, lime and limestone were transported by boat to Cagway Point from Port Henderson Hills, while bricks were manufactured both overseas and locally (initially at Spanish Town). A preliminary investigation of the fossil content of some of the blocks suggests that the Hellshire Hills – also referred to as Healthshire on early maps – might be another source.

BRICKS

Following the capture of Jamaica from the Spanish, the British lost no time in building fortifications to guard against the enemy. The first defensive breastwork at Port Royal commenced in 1656 and was known as Fort Cromwell, but was renamed Fort Charles in 1660. As noted previously, building bricks were manufactured locally, but when demand exceeded supply, ships coming to Jamaica were ordered to be ballasted with bricks. Portland cement was not invented until 1824, so the early builders used a mortar consisting chiefly of lime (calcium oxide), derived from burning limestone, together with sand and water and, occasionally, other substances, such as molasses and even fragments of pre-existing bricks. Such a mixture is extremely cohesive and durable and can bind bricks and other materials together for hundreds of years.

A close examination of the bricks at Port Royal reveals that they are predominantly red, but some are deep purple to grey-black, and glassy. Such bricks are the result of overheating, and some may have been deliberately burnt and then strategically placed in the walls to create a pattern. Many, however, appear to be the recycled remains of earlier bricks burnt in one or more of the disastrous fires that affected Port Royal in the eighteenth century. The yellow-brown stock bricks from London, which have also been used in restoration work at Fort Charles, are from a later period.

Texturally, some bricks are uniformly fine-grained and others are very coarse, with large pebble-sized fragments. Another important feature is the method used for laying bricks. In general, they are placed in horizontal layers, called courses, and bound together with mortar. The bricks are also arranged in patterns called bonds, and laid with either the short ends (headers) or long ends (stretchers) exposed (see chapter 2). The wall of the old Naval Dockyard is an excellent example of a red-brick structure with a Flemish bond, in which the headers and stretchers alternate. In addition, the capping on some walls consists of bricks placed lengthwise at an angle of forty-five degrees; and in some places, such as along the Town Line northeast of Fort Charles, one can still see bricks called Specials, with a curved outer surface. During the 1969–70 excavations, from the site of a pre-1692 church, Mayes recovered bricks that were glazed at one end, as well as ceramic tiles.[6] Generally speaking, most of the bricks still to be seen at Port Royal measure 9 × 4 × 2.5 inches (23 × 10 × 6.4 centimetres), but variations do occur.

OTHER BUILDING STONES

Some years ago, while carrying out a geological reconnaissance of Port Royal, I noticed that the light-buff to pale grey-brown slabs of a very fossil-rich limestone (Plate 3.1) that covered the floor of Fort Charles were unlike any other limestone recorded in Jamaica. Further examination revealed that it is composed of a very rich assemblage of tightly packed freshwater shells and shell fragments (Plate 3.2), and on the basis of a comparison with other known British building stones it was subsequently identified as Purbeck Limestone, from Dorset in England.[7] This beautiful stone, which dates back to near the end of the Jurassic Period (the age of the dinosaurs) about 140 million years ago, is to be found in many buildings throughout southern England, perhaps the most famous of which is Westminster Abbey.

Plate 3.1 Platform at Fort Charles paved with imported fossil-rich Purbeck limestone.

But the overseas export of British building stones with special qualities was very rare in the seventeenth century, and it would seem that Jamaica received special treatment from the king. As noted by Rowland Powell in letters written to William Coventry in 1679:

> Since the French alarmed this place the Inhabitants have laboured att the Fortificacons, they have layd the Free stone for Platforms w'ch the King sent to His Excellency, and are now raising of a Line with a Batterie of 12 demicanon behind the old Church, w'ch will much strengthen the Harbour. This comes by way of Bristoll, other shipps beeing in readiness within few days for London.[8]

A few days later Powell reported: "At the Point wee have made a good Platforme in Fort James with the Free stone the King was pleased to send, when I came over, and now they are att work on a Breastwork behind the old church in the cod of the Bay."[9]

At the beginning of 2004, it was not clear to me whether the "free stone" sent by the king before 1692 was in fact the same fossil-rich Purbeck stone that can still be seen today at Fort Charles. Then, while researching the records, I came across the following report submitted on 5 June 1686 by the committee appointed to view the fortifications of Port Royal:

> This day, in obedience to the order of this house, we (with a committee appointed by the council) have viewed the fortifications of Port-Royal, and find the same in so good a condition that they cannot be mended without making them new; all the platforms being well laid with purbeck stone, except the Diamond, at Fort-James, which is laid with plank, which as yet is reasonably good, but stones enough lie ready in the same fort to repair it when it decays.[10]

Although spared, Fort Charles was badly shaken in 1692, and it took several years to repair the damage. Between 1700 and 1725 many significant events occurred at Port Royal, among them a disastrous fire in 1702, and a recommendation by the House of Assembly in 1706 that a new jail be built. In the early 1720s, St Peter's Church was restored, the Hanover line west of Fort Charles (see Figure 3.3) had to be repaired and Fort Charles was extended. To carry out

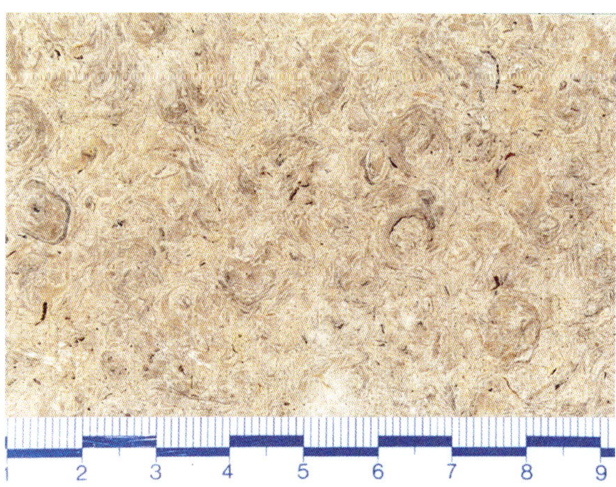

Plate 3.2 Close-up of Purbeck limestone showing texture and fossil content.

this work, it was reported, "There is sufficient quantity of Portland stones to pave both the Hanover line and the new addition to the fort when filled up."[11] Although similar in colour, Purbeck and Portland stones are very different in texture – and, therefore, easy to distinguish – but it has not yet been possible to examine every slab of stone at either site, so confirmation of the latter will have to wait until further work is undertaken.

Plate 3.3 Sandstone (Millstone Grit) copings resting on courses of white limestone. In the distance beyond the sea wall is the Coast Guard station at Port Royal.

In 1692 Fort James sank, along with two other fortifications, Fort Carlisle and Fort Rupert. Little was known about Fort Rupert until 1968, when a team of divers rediscovered a section of it submerged in the shallow lagoon located due east of Morgan's Harbour Hotel.[12] Should a more detailed investigation be undertaken of this historic site, it is almost certain that blocks of Purbeck stone will be uncovered among the fort's submerged remains.

What about the magnificent coping stones along the sea wall on the western (harbour) side of the old Naval Hospital building? These are prominently stratified, beige to pale golden-brown, coarse-grained slabs of sandstone that contain recognizable sub-rounded pea-sized grains of quartz in a sand-sized matrix of quartz and a few other minerals (Plate 3.3). As previously reported, the slabs are up to 7 feet (2.13 metres) long and 32 inches (81 centimetres) wide, and have a curved upper surface and a flat base with a maximum thickness of 11 inches (28 centimetres).[13] This humped type is a saddleback coping.

Geologically speaking, this sandstone occurs within the Millstone Grit Series. Whether the slabs were all cut to shape and then dressed in England before being shipped to Jamaica is still not clear. At either end of the wall, however, it forms a capping over red bricks, while in the central section of the wall it forms a capping over squared cut white limestone blocks.

Within the sea wall are two openings for jetties, which facilitated movement of people, water and supplies between the hospital and Kingston. Interestingly, the platform at each entrance is floored with large, coarse-grained slabs of granite (see Plate 1.2) containing prominent white rectangular crystals (phenocrysts) of the mineral feldspar. Further investigation of one of these crystals by X-ray methods reveals that the diffractogram is consistent with microcline, a potash feldspar. The larger of the two slabs is 72 inches (183 centimetres) long, 48 inches (122 centimetres) wide and 14 inches (36 centimetres) thick. No written records have yet been found stating the source of this material, but it is reminiscent of Cornish granite outcropping in southwest England that formed during Carboniferous times (called the Mississippian-Pennsylvanian periods in the United States). It is also unclear when these granite slabs were first shipped to Jamaica, as the discovery, in September 1859, of "a large granite stone somewhat the shape and size of a tombstone, which was covered with a coral formation, so that I could not tell whether it had an inscription on not" by naval diver Jeremiah Murphy, while exploring the sunken remains of old Fort James, raises the possibility that dressed granite might have been sent to Jamaica for building purposes much earlier than we think.[14]

Associated with the granite at the jetty is a fine-grained, pale green-grey to brown variety of sandstone, which splits uniformly along very thin strata called bedding planes. This variety of stone is from the Lower Coal Measures that outcrops in Yorkshire, England. It is commonly used for paving purposes and is known commercially as flagstone.

Table 3.1 Port Royal Building Stones

Materials	Principal Use	Place of Origin	Geologic Formation and Age	Remarks / Features
Bricks	Walls	Jamaica; England	Not applicable	Predominantly red or red-brown, some grey; texture coarse to fine
Limestone	Walls	Jamaica	Chiefy the Newport Formation, Lower Miocene (23–15 million years old)	White; massive, compact, finely crystalline; some with fossils
	Flooring	Dorset county, England	Purbeck Formation, Upper Jurassic or Lower Cretaceous (~140 million yr old)	Buff to pale grey; fresh-water limestone packed with the remains of gastropod shells
Marble	Wall plaques, monuments	Northern Tuscany	Of Triassic age, mainly from the Carrara region	Pure white in colour
	Flooring	Probably Devon, England, or Italy	To be determined	Mottled or veined, white to blue-grey
Granite	Flooring	Cornwall county (probably near Penryn), England	Probably Carbonlferous (350–285 mllllon years old)	Large, elongated crystals of potash feldspar (2 cm)
Sandstone	Coping stone (wall cappings)	Yorkshire, England	Millstone Grit Series, from the Namurian Epoch (Upper Carboniferous); about 320 million years old	Medium- to coarse-grained; straw- to honey-coloured; layering (bedding) prominent
	Flooring, steps, outdoor paving, foundations	Yorkshire, England (probably around Elland)	Probably Elland flagstone, of the Lower Coal Measures sequence, about 300 million years old (Upper Carboniferous)	Buff to pale yellowish-brown; fine-grained, with visible flakes of shiny, platy mica; well bedded
	Flooring and outdoor paving	Various localities in England	From the Old Red Sandstone (Devonian) to the New Red Sandstone (Permian)	Grey-green to greenish-grey; orange-red; pale yellow-brown

Table 3.1 continues

Table 3.1 continued

Slate	Roofing	Penrhyn quarry, North Wales	Cambrian (500 million years old)	Slaty cleavage; purplish; very fine-grained
		The Ffestiniog Belt, North Wales Delabole quarry (Cornwall) or the Cumbria area (Lake District)	Ordovician (400 million years old) Unknown	Slaty cleavage; blue-grey; very fine-grained Slaty cleavage; greenish; very fine-grained
	Flooring; probably other uses	Either England or Wales	To be determined	Large slabs with pale green, oval-shaped eye-like structures, composed of chlorite and other minerals; found in the old Naval Dockyard and elsewhere
Mortar	Binding agent	Jamaica	Not applicable	Composed of lime, mixed with sand (or gravel) and water

Other notable rock types to be seen at Port Royal (see Table 3.1) include the following:

1. Off-white and pale blue-grey marble tiles on the floor of St Peter's Church, which date back to at least 1725; both colours are suspected to be from Massa Carrara province in Italy.

2. White Carrara marble monuments on the wall of the church, and the Galdy tomb.

3. Light grey-green and purplish roofing slate, imported in the early 1800s, on a few of the still erect ancillary buildings at the old Naval Hospital. Geologically speaking, the slates found here (and elsewhere in Jamaica) range in age from 300 to 500 million years. These are probably the oldest type of rock imported for building purposes – some coming from the Penrhyn quarry in Wales and some from other quarry sites, possibly Delabole, in southwest England.

4. Large rectangular slabs of grey slate, measuring up to 7 feet (2.13 metres) in length and 1 inch (2.54 centimetres) thick, in a section of the old Naval Dockyard; most have been removed and are no doubt in use elsewhere in the island.

5. Slabs of Purbeck stone, similar to those on the platform at Fort Charles, in a drainage canal at the northwest corner of the old Naval Dockyard.

6. Loose fragments of chert and flint on the ground and below the surface. Some are local in origin, and some were imported as gunflints (see chapter 7).

THE COASTLINE

Another little-known and insufficiently appreciated feature of Port Royal is the extensive tract of land that has been built up by deposition since the great earthquake of 1692. At the time of the earthquake the town occupied an area of about

Plate 3.4 The eastern end of Kingston Harbour and the Palisadoes spit in 1774. Reproduced from a map dated 1 June 1774, facing p. 102 in Edward Long's *History of Jamaica*, vol. 2. (Depth in fathoms.)

60 acres (24 hectares), but much of this sank, leaving only about 25 acres (10 hectares) of dry surface area.[15] One of the consequences of this was the further isolation of the Port Royal cay, as a large gap of shallow water (several hundred metres wide) separated the surviving town from the rest of the Palisadoes spit. With the passage of time, the gap slowly began to fill in by the natural deposition of sand and gravel, but this process was aided by the residents of Port Royal, who sank old naval vessels and boats loaded with stones to speed up the process of accretion.

In 1725, Port Royal was bounded and protected on the westernmost side by the Hanover line, but a part of the line was being undermined by the sea and in danger of being lost unless speedily repaired.[16] By 1749, marine erosion seems to have given way to deposition, since the platform of the Hanover line had to be raised owing to the fact that "few of the guns of that battery are capable of striking the hull of a ship, by reason of the sand being thrown by the sea, higher than several of the guns".[17] Surviving maps show that, at the western end of the peninsula, Port Royal cay remained unconnected above sea level until about the mid-1700s, when sand began to appear above water, and that in 1774 at the eastern end, not far from Harbour Head, the Palisadoes spit was breached and a very narrow, unnavigable channel connected Kingston Harbour with the open sea (Plate 3.4). As noted by Long,

Plate 3.5 Aerial view of the western end of Port Royal, showing Fort Charles stranded inland. Photograph taken by the author in 2001.

> The broadest part of Port Royal peninsula is nearly opposite the East quarter of Kingston: on this part is a small grass-penn, stocked with sheep and goats. The side next the harbour is intersected with several little ponds and inlets; and here is the usual careening-place for merchant-ships. This neck of land might be made very passable for horses; but the people of Port Royal prefer a water-carriage, which is more pleasant, and equally expeditious.[18]

Since then deposition of sand and gravel has continued to rapidly transform the western end: the most dramatic effect of this activity is best illustrated by the present position of Fort Charles, which in 1692 was situated between the sea and Chocolata Hole, with the waves lapping at or near the base of the outer wall (built on beach rock) and facing Gun Cay. Today Fort Charles is stranded inland, with the coastline now lying approximately 1,000 feet (about 300 metres) to the southeast (Plate 3.5). The map of Port Royal (Figure 3.2) shows the position of the coastline before 1692 and at various intervals since then up to the present day. It is estimated that between 1692 and 2005 – a period of 313 years – more than 95 acres (38 hectares) have been built up in the region extending south and southwest from the lagoon to the coastline near the Coast Guard base. As a consequence, the gap between Port Royal and Gun Cay has narrowed considerably, and in time – probably in another four hundred years – Gun Cay and other coral banks could be joined to the mainland.

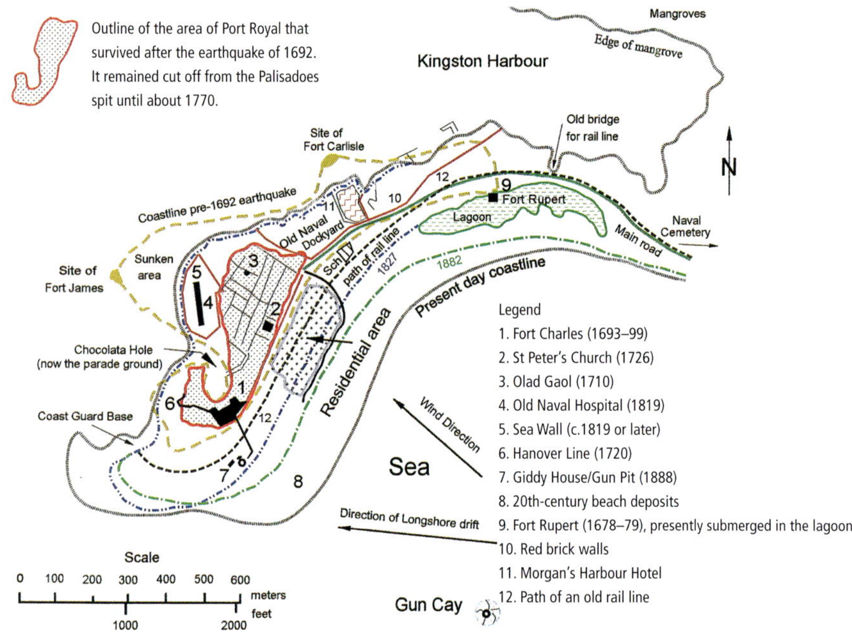

Note: Present-day coastline and points of interest are taken from late-twentieth-century aerial photographs. Earlier coastline positions, surveyed areas and physical features are taken from the map of Port Royal surveyed in June 1827 by Philip A. Morris, Crown surveyor, and from maps of Port Royal and Kingston Harbour surveyed by the British between 1873 and 1914.

Figure 3.2 Geo-historical map of Port Royal.

However, there is overwhelming evidence to support the view that global warming has begun and will cause sea levels to rise. One of the many outcomes of this climatic change will be the inundation of beaches, cays and other low-lying areas along the coastline.

RAIL LINE AND HOUSING

In the early 1880s, plans to further strengthen the defences of Port Royal were implemented. These included the Rocky Point Fort (to the east of the Naval Cemetery) and the Prince Albert and Victoria batteries. The latter, including the Royal Artillery Store, Gun Pit and concrete parapet wall, were then sited close to the shoreline, which extended southeast to more than 300 feet (about 100 metres) from the front of Fort Charles. At that time there was no road along the Palisadoes spit, and it was not until 1936 that a road leading to the airport and the lighthouse was finally opened.

The British installed a light rail system (see alignment on Figure 3.2) to move the huge coastal guns, ammunition, men and building materials from the shoreline inland, over the unconsolidated beach sand and gravel deposits. In 1907 the rail system, known as the "Permanent way", was buckled (Plate 3.6) by the same

Plate 3.6 Rail line called the Permanent Way, damaged by the earthquake in 1907. Reproduced from a Gardner Series postcard.

earthquake that triggered the liquefaction of the sand that caused the Giddy House to tilt at an angle of approximately seventeen degrees from the vertical. Today, very little of the rail line remains in place. However, it has been suggested by Panning that if Port Royal should ever be restored and marketed as a historic attraction, another rail system could be included as part of the tourism package (as is done in many theme parks worldwide).[19]

Since the 1960s part of the land east of St Peter's Church has been used for housing, thereby satisfying an immediate social need. This area, however, is totally unprotected from heavy winds, storm surge caused by tropical storms and hurricanes, and tsunami (great sea waves caused by submarine earthquakes or volcanic activity). For example, it was reported that on 28 August 1722 there was a "dreadful hurricane", which took nearly four hundred lives. "The new erected line on Port Royall call'd Hanover line stood it the best and as I am informed has been of great security to the remaining part of that town, which otherwise must have been destroyed by the breaking in of the sea upon them."[20] At the eastward part of the town the prodigious swell of the sea resulted in "several hundred tons of rocks of large size" being thrown up over the wall. Although Port Royal was mercifully spared during the passage of hurricane Ivan on 11 September 2004, the large volume of sand heaved up by the raging surf along the eastern section of the Palisadoes spit is a stark reminder of how it was formed, and the dangers faced by those who choose to live close to the coast.

HERITAGE TOURISM

Once ranked among the Western world's richest and wickedest towns, Port Royal is today a shadow of its former self. For many years Fort Charles has been the only historic building open to the public on a daily basis; its main features are shown in Figure 3.3. But there are

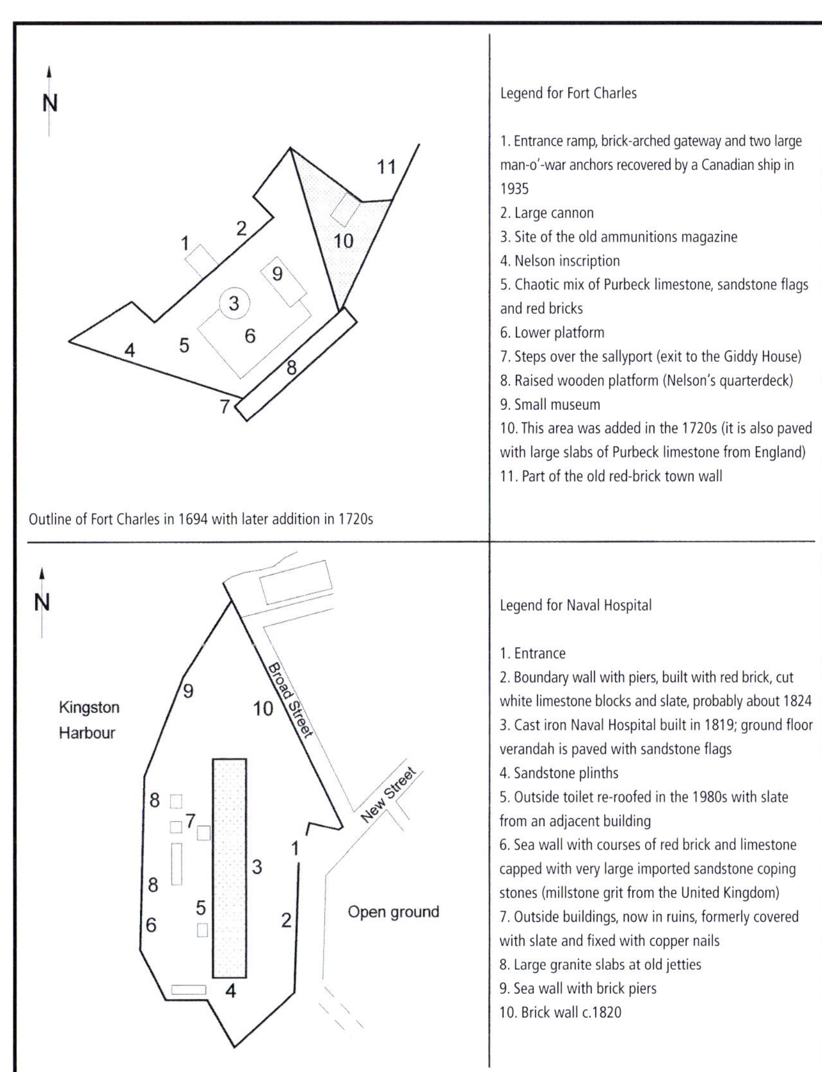

Figure 3.3 Plan views of Fort Charles and the old Naval Hospital.

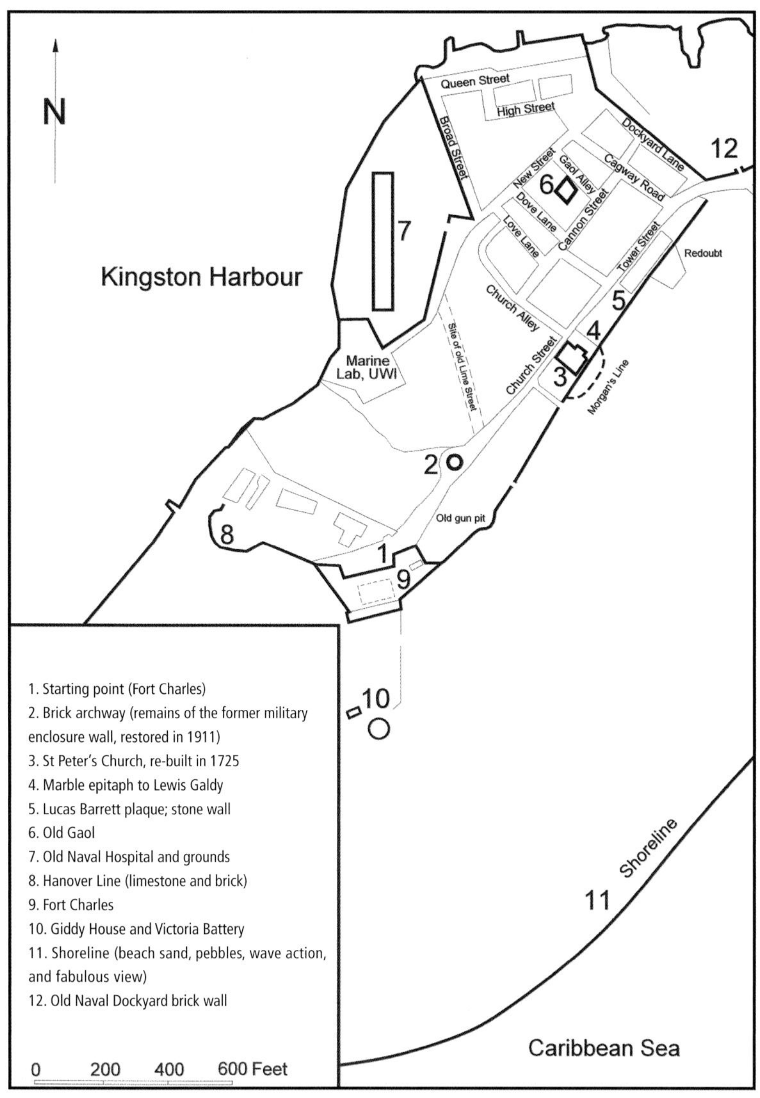

Figure 3.4 Port Royal geo-heritage walking-tour guide.

several other places and points of interest that could be included in a formal guided walking tour around the town (see Figure 3.4). Such an event, advertised as "a geo-heritage walking tour of Port Royal", was conducted by the Geological Society of Jamaica in December 2005 with great success.[21] This popular tour was part of the activities planned by the society to celebrate its fiftieth anniversary and, until an illustrated guidebook on the heritage-tourism potential of Port Royal is written and available to the general public, it is hoped that the field guide for that tour, together with this book, will provide useful references for those who may wish to explore on their own.

4

Fort Augusta Revisited

Extending from the foot of the Port Henderson hills in a northeasterly direction for approximately 2.25 miles (3.6 kilometres) is a narrow strip of land that separates an area of shoals and swamp (which was partly reclaimed in the late 1960s and now forms part of Portmore) from Kingston Harbour. At the tip of this peninsula stands Fort Augusta, the largest and most formidable fortress or stronghold ever constructed in Jamaica, and, arguably, the most elaborate and extraordinary piece of eighteenth-century architecture still standing in the island.

This stretch of land consists largely of a mixture of sediment (sand, silt and organic matter) brought in from the northwest by the Rio Cobre and sand deposited by the combined action of wind, waves and currents from the southeast. According to the records, one of the most significant effects of the 1692 earthquake that devastated Port Royal was the sudden change in the position of the channel.[1] Previously, any ship entering the harbour had to pass in front of the guns mounted in Fort Charles (and three other forts which sank – Forts James, Carlisle and Rupert), but after the catastrophic event, bathymetric surveys and soundings revealed the presence of a new channel (Plate 4.1). Simply speaking, the seismic shocks triggered changes in the bottom topography, resulting in a deepening of the channel along the western edge of the harbour. As a consequence, Port Royal was now much more vulnerable: with only Fort Charles still remaining above ground, any enemy ship could pass by freely without coming within effective range of its guns. In contrast, the end of the narrow peninsula

Plate 4.1 Fort Augusta and its relationship to the channel into Kingston Harbour. Reproduced from a map dated 1 June 1774, facing p. 102 in Long, *History of Jamaica*, vol. 2. (Depth in fathoms.)

(then called Mosquito-Point) now lay adjacent to the newly created channel and was considered a strategic site, as noted in the records of the House of Assembly: "Mosquito-Point may be proper to build a fort at, if the foundation be good, but in regard of its unhealthy situation, and for saving money, I do imagine that a floating battery may be more proper for that place, and much cheaper, and also removable upon any occasion."[2]

But it appears that no further action was taken until the late 1730s, when, with the worsening of relations between Britian and Spain, the island's governing bodies agreed that "a battery of guns, at or near Mosquito-Point is necessary, and would be a great defence to the harbours of Port-Royal and Kingston, and the island in general".[3] Thus, in an effort to strengthen the southern approaches into Kingston Harbour, work finally began on the erection of a fort at Mosquito-Point in 1740. Geometrically, the fort is a five-sided polygon, at the corners of which are four-sided outward extensions called bastions, and each is connected by curtain walls. Capping the curtains and bastions on the western and southern sides is a low wall in which there are regularly spaced openings, called crenels (or embrasures), and solid uprights, called merlons. This protective barrier through which the guns are fired is known as the battlement.

The fort is approximately 1,200 feet (366 metres) long by 600 feet (183 metres) across at the widest point, and covers some 12 acres (almost 5 hectares). It was designed and constructed to house ninety 24-pounder guns. To support this substantial structure, piles of palmetto and pigeon wood, up to 18 feet (5.5 metres) in length, had to be driven into the ground until a firm layer was encountered. In addition to the physical difficulties posed by the terrain, those who laboured in the construction of this fortress had to contend with mosquito-borne illnesses, fever, heat, inadequate supplies of drinking water and hurricanes, one of which, in 1744, wiped out most of what had been built up until then.

CONSTRUCTION PERIOD, 1745–1760

Despite these setbacks, orders were given to carry on, and the following passages, taken from the *Journal of the Assembly of Jamaica,* provide insight into some of the major hurdles that had to be overcome in preparing the site for the fort at Mosquito-Point.[4]

> There will be 33 carriages for guns necessary to be made, and they were ordered so to be by his excellency in writing, on the 11th June, 1748; the timber and materials for which are in place; . . .
>
> There hath been a very great quantity of firm solid land made by Mr Beckford, in pursuance of his contract, out of the lagoon; which land he hath made 20 feet wider than he agreed, on the whole length of the line, which is 320 feet; and the said land so made is, by what appears to the committees, about four feet in thickness: The committees are of opinion, that such addition of land was absolutely necessary, to enlarge the esplanade of the fort; which otherwise would have been too small and confined, and was, as they are informed, directed by his excellency the governor.
>
> The new works next the land and lagoon are near finished, being of earth, and are ten feet high above the water . . .
>
> The committees observed, that Mr Beckford, the contractor, hath been under very great and unforeseen difficulties, in making the ground aforementioned, out of the lagoon; and erecting the said works of earth, by being obliged, at a very great expence, to make a navigable canal, of more than a quarter of a mile in length, and of preparing boats to fetch sand by the said canal; for the land directly in front of the fort belongs to the office of ordnance, and there have been constantly upon it magazines of gunpowder, and of filled shells and other ordnance stores; and the next lot to that land belongs to Mr Solomon Boussart, who, as the committees were informed, absolutely refused to let any of Mr Beckford's agents take any from thence, so that they were under a necessity of going as far as the sand hills to get any, and to make the said canal for the conveniency of bringing it.

Among the materials used in its construction between 1 October 1753 and 31 December 1754 were the following: 333,200 English bricks (of which 10,000 were Bridgewater bricks); 10,000 tons of white limestone from Salt-Pond-Hill (now known as Port Henderson Hill); 24 tons of Bath stone; 2,500 flagstones; 1,074 tons of sand; a large amount of lime (including 60 sugar hogshead of Bristol lime and 47 sugar hogshead of Plymouth lime) and 11,142 pigeonwood and palmetto piles.[5] According to the joint committees there was no defect in any part of the work performed,

> except the cordon at Mosquito-Point that is made of Port Antonio stone, which, by being exposed to the spray of the sea, mouldereth away; this defect may be easily remedied at a small expence, by taking out the bad stone, and putting Bath stone, which is soon expected from England in the stead thereof.[6]

Although it has been reported by Cundall[7] and others that the fort was erected in 1753, it is clear from the records that in January 1756 it was still incomplete.

> The joint committees of the council and of the house, find, at Fort-Augusta or Mosquito-Point, that the face, orillon, flank, and half the curtain, of the works towards a place called the Admiralty-Ground, are raised up to the cordon, but no merlons, and that the other half of the curtain, flank, orillon, and face, is all piled, and part of the foundation raised: That the ditch is almost finished, with one half of the counterscarp wall . . . The joint committees are of opinion, that Fort-Augusta ought to be finished and completed, as soon as possible, as it is of the utmost consequence to the security of the island.[8]

In 1756 this military fortification was renamed Fort Augusta, in honour of the mother of King George III.

In October 1759, almost four years later, much still remained to be done, as shown by a detailed estimate of the work proposed to complete Fort-Augusta at "Musquito-Point", which stated:

> 10,987 ton of stone, . . . 4,400 hogsheads of lime, . . . 2,000 tons of fresh water sand, . . . 1000 piles for the foundation, from C to D, . . . 49 merlons towards the channel, to be according to the plan and profile, faced with large hewn free-stone, from the cordon, 12,939 feet stone, and finished for laying, . . . and 32 merlons towards the land.[9]

CONSTRUCTION PERIOD, 1761–1900

On 14 September 1763 the magazine, containing three hundred barrels of powder, was struck by lightning, resulting in a huge explosion. The extent of the damage was clearly described in the *Journal of Assembly of Jamaica.*

> The magazine is entirely blown up and destroyed, and no part of the materials to be found. . . . The officers barracks demolished; a very small part of the materials are remaining, that can be made useful towards re-building the same. . . . The wall which inclosed the magazine all down; a few of the stones left. . . . The north flank of the fortification, next to the magazine, so much shaken, that it must be pulled down . . . There are sundry damages done to the platforms, merlons, etc, which the committees cannot precisely estimate. . . . Where the magazine stood, there is a large pool of water; which the committees are of opinion should be filled up. . . . The joint committees are of opinion, that there will be no occasion to re-build the north flank of the fortification.[10]

During the mid-1770s, strengthening of the fort was still underway. It was being constructed to support ninety 24-pounders.[11] By 1777, following steady progress, the following was reported to have been done.

> The brow to the lagoon bastion is finished, and an arch turned over the land-port gate, to join the half curtains: Two bomb-proofs are finished; and the lagoon bastion, and half curtain, appear to the joint committee to be two-thirds finished. . . . The magazine is enclosed with a wall, within which is a convenient yard for airing the powder; and the rooms for weighing, sifting, and coopering the same are finished . . . and a wharf is likewise nearly finished, for landing the powder from the boats: . . . A cistern is made to contain the water brought from the river, for the use of the fort.[12]

The following year the committee recommended that the wharf at the sally-port be lengthened, because the water had become too shallow for loaded boats to come to it; that banquettes should be made between the guns; and that the merlons on the lagoon bastion be raised. It was further suggested "that three cuts, from sea to sea, between Port-Henderson and Fort-Augusta, supported by small pieces of artillery, should be immediately made, to impede the approaches of an enemy".[13]

On 30 July 1784 further structural damage was inflicted on the fort by the passage of a storm that destroyed the hospital and caused the salient angle of the north bastion to sink upwards of 3 feet, because the foundation was bad.[14]

On 27 May 1808 a mutiny took place in the Second West-India Regiment at Fort Augusta, resulting in the death of two officers and several mutineers. The committee that was appointed to make an enquiry into the circumstances reported that "it was not by any means confined to a mutiny among the recruits, but that many of the old soldiers, if not openly and directly concerned in it, did persuade and excite the recruits to mutiny".[15]

FORT AUGUSTA SINCE 1900

Fort Augusta has always been surrounded on all sides by water except for the sandy stretch of land to the west. To protect this section against ground attack, a ditch was dug and a ravelin constructed on the outside of the main wall. The land to the west belonged to the Admiralty and was used initially for naval stores and later as a military cemetery.

What is not widely known, however, is that during an eight-month period between 1915 and 1916 a feature film, *The Daughter of the Gods,* starring Annette Kellerman, was shot in Jamaica by Fox Film Corporation, and one of the main locations was Fort Augusta. In bidding farewell to the people of Jamaica in April 1916, Mr Herbert Brenon, the director, remarked, "It has been my duty to handle many thousands some days at

Fort Augusta, so all told I have handled close to 150,000. This is no exaggeration when one thinks of the many days when I had 3,000 at a time. To these men I send my message of thanks."[16] Unfortunately, this ten-reel black-and-white film from the silent-era days is listed as lost, since no copy is known to exist, although one reel is believed to be present in a Russian archive. The movie is said to have cost about US$1 million

Plate 4.2 Aerial view of Fort Augusta as it appeared in 1949.
Source: Huntings Aerosurveys, Flight N\Jam\49, Line 12, Frame 6.

to produce, and the studio head, William Fox, was allegedly so incensed that he removed Brenon's name from the list of credits, but Brenon sued and won.[17]

Aerial photographs taken of Fort Augusta in 1949 by Hunting Aerosurveys Limited clearly show breaches in the perimeter wall on the north side, partial inundation of the parade ground on the south side and heavy overgrowth in some places (Plate 4.2).[18] The original structure, however, remained essentially intact, and in 1952 the War Department transferred the historic ruins and site to the Government of Jamaica.[19]

Although few buildings were of use, the boundary walls were in fair condition, so the government decided to convert the site into a prison to alleviate the problem of gross overcrowding in the General Penitentiary in Kingston and the St Catherine District Prison. At that time access to the

Plate 4.3 Main entrance to Fort Augusta.

fort was by sea, as the road from Port Henderson had not been built. To aid in the reconstruction process, the government approved an expenditure of £21,000, and boatloads of prisoners were transported daily to the fort by launch to carry out repairs, build dormitories and undertake other forms of work. By the end of March 1955 the first dormitory had been completed and was occupied by 28 prisoners. The plan was to construct ten dormitories to accommodate 280 male prisoners.[20]

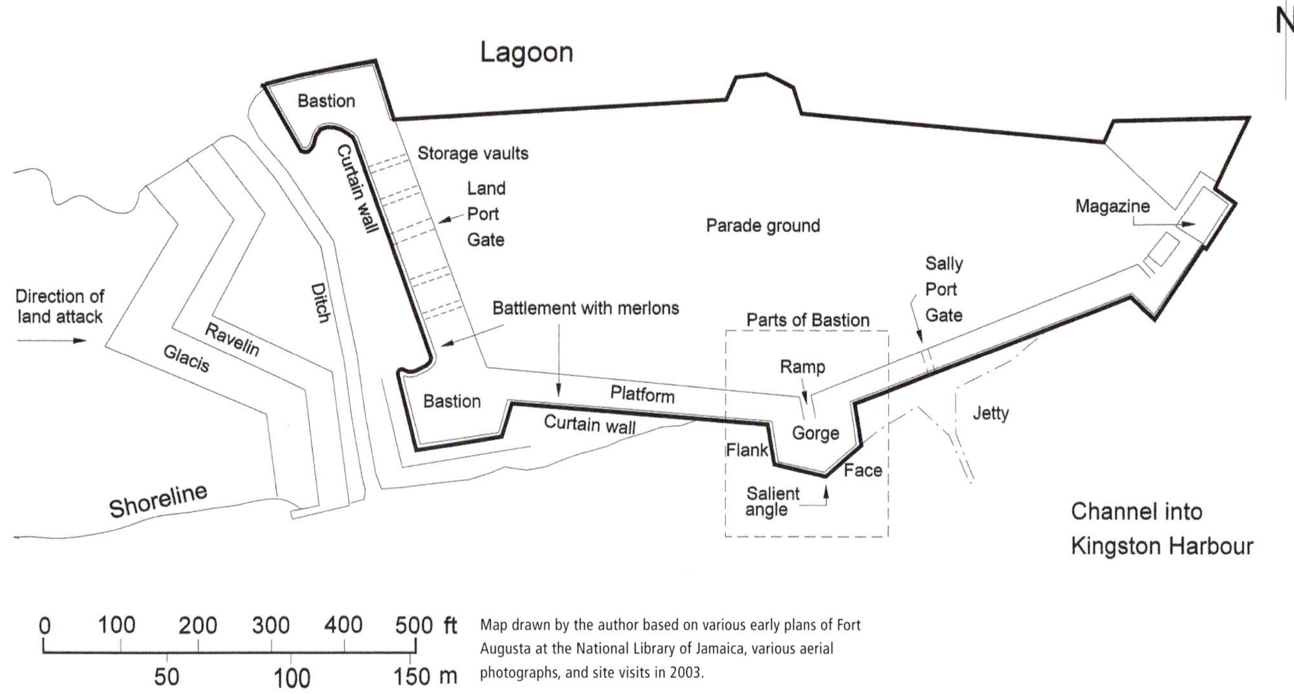

Figure 4.1 Main structural features of Fort Augusta.

In 1957, the Historical Society of Jamaica toured the fort, with the then director of prisons, Mr I. Childs, as their guide. At that time there were one hundred male prisoners working under the direction of warders, re-laying bricks in crumbling walls, rebuilding arches, infilling cracks and repositioning worn flagstones where necessary. Within the walls of the fort, modern reinforced buildings were under construction. Those that had been completed included one wing of dormitories and a large tiled kitchen and cookout. The plan for the intact powder magazines at the northeast end was to convert the larger one with very thick walls into a chapel, and the other into a storeroom.[21]

Fort Augusta remained a detention centre for male prisoners for more than thirty years. Then in February 1988, the St Jago Female Institution on Monk Street in Spanish Town was closed and all female prisoners were transferred to Fort Augusta. Since then the fort has served as a correctional centre for females only, but it has now been acquired by the Port Authority of Jamaica, and although this organization plans to build a terminal at the northern end to facilitate its shipping operations in Kingston Harbour, it will retain the structure as a heritage site.

Today, approaching Fort Augusta from the west, the unpaved road passes through the old cemetery (although all visible signs have long since disappeared) and over a gently elevated breach in the apex of the V-shaped walls of the ravelin, before reaching the main entrance to this formidable battlemented structure (Plate 4.3). Should it be possible one day soon to convert Fort Augusta into a visitor attraction, there are a number of interesting features that still survive and which could form part of a guided walking tour (Figure 4.1).

WESTERN END

On the western end is an impressive vertical wall consisting of twenty-two courses of cut white limestone blocks, each approximately 9 inches (22.8 centimetres) in

Plate 4.4 The western approach to Fort Augusta as seen through a red-bricked embrasure. Port Henderson Hill and the walled ravelin are clearly visible.

height. On top of this is a crenulated parapet wall consisting of red brick merlons, and openings called embrasures, behind which the 24-pounder guns were placed (Plate 4.4). In the centre of the wall at ground level is Land Port Gate, a semi-cylindrical passage with parallel abutments, about 55 feet (17 metres) long, through which everyone must pass to gain entry into the walled enclosure. The total height of the wall – from ground surface to the top of the merlon – at this spot is about 20 feet (6 metres). Within the body of the wall are four tunnel vaults (or arched chambers), which were used for storage. At both corners of this massive wall are two polygon-shaped structures called bastions. Unfortunately, the development of several large cracks in the outer face of the northwest bastion poses a serious threat, and corrective action needs to be undertaken swiftly if it is to be preserved.

SOUTHERN SIDE

On the southern side, facing the channel and extending from the southwest bastion to the eastern end, is the longest section of battlement wall. It contains fifty-five embrasures, including twelve in the central bastion. The top of the parapet is approximately 8.5 feet (2.59 metres) thick, and behind it is the continuation of

Plate 4.5 Large, hewn blocks of imported Bath stone form part of the parapet wall in the central bastion. The rusting cannon is a relic of a bygone era.

the very wide platform, paved with slabs of Purbeck limestone shading in colour from white to light buff, and sandstone flagstones of maroon and pale green to grey. From a geo-historical perspective, however, perhaps the most interesting part of the fort is the central bastion, the wall of which consists of a mix of red bricks, blocks of local cut white limestone, and large blocks and slabs of imported dressed white limestone up to 9 inches (22.8 centimetres) thick. This material is a naturally occurring fine-grained limestone characterized by its oolitic texture and cream-to-buff colour, which mellows on exposure to pale yellow or light honey-brown (Plate 4.5). It was deposited during Middle Jurassic times (about 150 million years ago) and is obtained from quarries on the outskirts of Bath in the county of Somerset, hence the name Bath stone. It has been used in the construction of many famous buildings, including Windsor Castle and Longleat House in Wiltshire.

Of particular interest at Fort Augusta are the carved initials and dates of several servicemen stationed there in 1760. And behind the embrasures are semicircular platforms constructed with truncated, wedge-shaped slabs of very fossiliferous Purbeck limestone measuring up to 22 inches (56 centimetres) in width. A brick-walled ramp leads from the gorge down to the parade (ground level), but this route has been fenced off and grill-gated since the mid-1950s. To the immediate east of the central bastion are: a small conical red-brick tower, called a turret, with a single loophole; a platform covered by red bricks with an interesting herringbone pattern in the centre that points to the loophole; the jetty, where stores and personnel were loaded and offloaded; and the ground-level passageway known as the Sally Port. This, too, has also been blocked off, but the remains of part of the jetty can still be seen.

Plate 4.6 The military magazine houses several brick-lined barrel vaults. It was used at one time by the British as a chapel.

EASTERN END

Following the explosion of three hundred barrels of powder stored in a magazine that was struck by lightning on 14 September 1763, a new magazine was completed in 1764. It was built with red brick and blocks of cut white limestone (Plate 4.6), and the interior consists of thick-walled barrel vaults and a large central room. In the late 1950s, tomb plaques were salvaged from the old military cemetery and inlaid in the interior walls and floors. In 1960, the task of converting the old military magazine into a chapel was finally completed.[22] One of the marble inscriptions on the wall is to the memory of Captain Joseph Greenwood of His Majesty's Twenty-second Regiment "who departed this life at Fort Augusta 31st October 1828 Aged 32 years", and on the floor is a large grey tombstone dated 1810. Among the more recent memorials is one to Gunner Joseph James Horton of the Sixty-six Company R.G.A., who "Died at Port Royal, 1st December 1904 Aged 26 years". Another one, to David Bruce Gordon, who died on 4 March 1916 at 24 years of age, was "Erected by the officers and crew Australian ship, Melbourne".

NORTHERN WALL

Nothing remains today of the original wall. What existed in 1949 was largely in ruins, and the whole line was subsequently replaced with concrete and cement when the fort was converted to a prison.

5

Pre-Columbian Stone Artefacts

A large number of smoothly ground, often very highly polished, tear-shaped or axe-like, chisel-edged stone implements, known as petaloid celts, have been found at numerous sites throughout Jamaica. They are among the best-preserved artefacts left behind by the original inhabitants of the island, called the Tainos (formerly known as the Arawaks). The origin of the Tainos has been traced by means of the distinctive pottery they made to the banks of the Orinoco River in Venezuela, from where they moved outwards to the Guianas and Trinidad and thence northwards to the Greater Antilles, which they colonized around AD 600.

One of the earliest published references to the existence of pre-Columbian stone artefacts in Jamaica is that of P. Browne in 1756, who stated:

> The third is the produce of some other country; and has been introduced here, very much in the time of the native Indians, who used to grind their maize with those small figured masses, which we call thunderbolts: It was manufactured in some part of the neighbouring continent and worked into various forms to supply those people with tools for the different occasions of life, while the nature and manufacture of iron was yet unknown to them.[1]

In November 1895, the then curator of the Institute of Jamaica, Dr J.E. Duerden, assembled a large collection of these and described them in a very informative paper entitled "Aboriginal Indian Remains in Jamaica", published in 1897. He concluded: "The most abundant material undoubtedly belongs to the trappean series of rocks, including the trachytes, felsites, rhyolites and basalts so prominent in various parts of the island."[2] His rock identification was based essentially on a visual examination of many of the almost four hundred celts in the collection. Today, his "trappean series" would be simply grouped under the heading "lava", which refers to certain types of extrusive (volcanic) igneous rocks.

In the early 1970s, a, largely non-destructive examination of 458 such objects was undertaken by Dr John Roobol (a lecturer in the Department of Geology at University of the West Indies) and Dr James Lee (president of the Archaeological Society of Jamaica).[3] The results of their study showed that while the three major classes of rocks – igneous, sedimentary and metamorphic – were represented, 78 per cent of these stone artefacts were classified as greenstone. This is a term applied to extremely fine-grained, massive, greenish-coloured rocks lacking visible structure that have been lightly metamorphosed. The specimens for this study came chiefly from two collections: the Bond Collection, comprising 66 celts, housed at the Institute of Jamaica, and the James Lee collection, comprising 359 celts, which he amassed between the early 1950s and the early 1970s.

Table 5.1 Lithological Celt Types Found in Jamaica

Rock Class	Name	Number	Percentage
Metamorphic	Greenstone	357	79.2
	Blackstone	42	9.3
	White schist	6	1.3
	Blue schist	3	0.7
Other	Lava	24	5.3
	Sedimentary rock	14	3.1
	Conch shell	3	0.7
	Mineral	2	0.4
Total		451	100.0

Source: Derived from M.J. Roobol and J.W. Lee, "Petrography and Source of Some Arawak Rock Artifacts from Jamaica" (paper presented at the Sixth Congrès Internacional pour l'Étude des Cultures Pre-Columbiennes des Petites Antilles, Guadeloupe, 1975), 304–13.

The authors arrived at the following conclusions:

> All of the artefacts so far described were manufactured from rocks and minerals common to Jamaica. This does not prove that they originated in Jamaica, as the geology of this island is similar to that of Hispaniola and Puerto Rico. Only two artefacts were found composed of rock which can be proven to have originated outside of Jamaica. [These two are] composed of granular quartzite.[4]

In summary, they state: "Around 90% of the artifacts are manufactured from low-grade metamorphic rocks of which greenstone predominates."[5] They recognized eight lithological types, as summarized in Table 5.1. The method they used to obtain the above results was described as follows:

> In the first instance a collection of 22 broken petaloid tools was examined. As these proved to be extremely fine grained, slices were cut from them and prepared for microscopic examination. Having identified the main rock types with certainty it was then possible to identify further specimens without damage by hand lenses or binocular microscope examination of a wet surface. Many specimens required scrubbing prior to this examination to remove surface encrustation.[6]

RESULTS OF PRESENT STUDY

Following the discovery of commercial-grade bauxite in Jamaica in the early 1940s, three North American companies, namely Alcan, Kaiser and Reynolds, commenced exploration activities in the parishes of Manchester, St Ann and St Elizabeth. At that time the composition and depth of the ore were ascertained by a combination of manually dug pits and hand-augered drill holes. In the more remote areas, such as at St Toolies in the Harmon's Valley area of Manchester parish (Figure 5.1), field offices were set up and many local residents were hired. In an effort to secure employment, several applicants brought forth petaloid celts and offered them as gifts.[7] These had been preserved over the years by placing them at the bottom of water storage jars, where it was believed that they would keep the water cool. This custom served the dual role of safeguarding the celts and keeping them in mint condition. Interestingly, many appear never to have been used as cutting tools, a fact that has led many archaeologists to believe that they were a highly prized trade item, possibly used as a gift or as a form of currency.

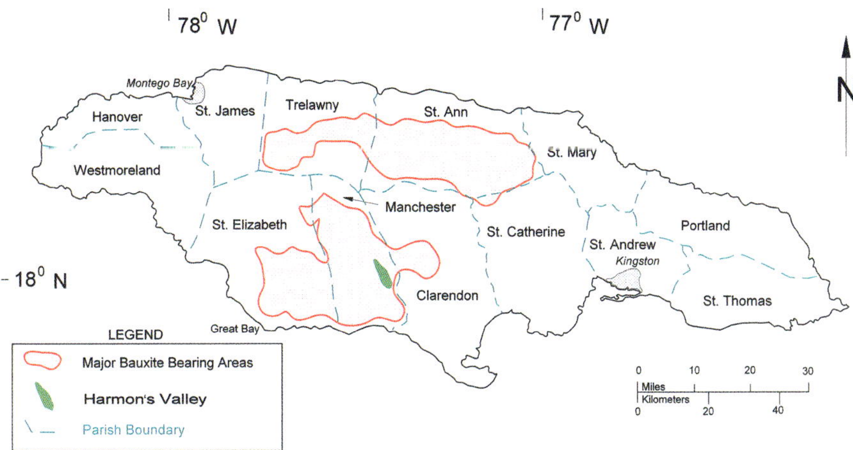

Figure 5.1 Location of Harmon's Valley in Manchester parish.

One of the great difficulties that one experiences in undertaking studies of highly polished celts is that the true texture is often not visible. As a consequence, is it virtually impossible to ascertain the true nature and geological origin of some of these celts. The present study of one particular specimen, found in Harmon's Valley in the parish of Manchester in central Jamaica, highlights the difficulty. Externally the celt is reddish-brown in colour and cannot, therefore, be classified as either greenstone or blackstone. However, when sawn in half the interior can be seen to be uniformly green (Plate 5.1) and composed of very tightly interlocking, fine-grained crystals with a vitreous lustre, embedded within which are small disseminated grains of another mineral with a brassy metallic lustre (Plate 5.2). The true colour and texture of the original rock was masked by a thin, highly polished outer surface that consists in part of iron oxide. As a consequence,

Plate 5.1 Two jadeite celts, probably imported from Central America. The lower celt was sawn in half using a special diamond-studded rock-cutting blade.

Plate 5.2 Close-up view of the cut surface showing disseminated grains of brassy-coloured pyrite embedded in a tightly interlocking mass of jadeite crystals. Scale in millimetres.

other investigative techniques were undertaken to characterize the celt. These included, first of all, making a thin section (0.03 millimetres in thickness) from a cut slice for further examination under polarized light. Another piece, about the size of a Jamaican twenty-dollar coin and weighing almost 10 grams, was pulverized and divided into two portions – one to determine its chemical composition by X-ray fluorescence (XRF) and the other to ascertain its X-ray diffraction (XRD) pattern.

Plate 5.3 Microscopic detail of the celt viewed in plane-polarized light. The opaque mineral (1.0 millimetres diameter) in the top left-hand corner is pyrite (magnification × 10).

With the aid of the microscope, the specimen can be seen to consist largely of tightly interlocking granular crystals of a pyroxene mineral altering to a fibrous amphibole mineral, either uralite or actinolite (Plates 5.3 and 5.4). Associated with this assemblage are small (about 1 millimetre in diameter) disseminated grains of opaque pyrite, which in reflected light has a brassy, metallic lustre. Further studies by

Plate 5.4 Microscopic detail of the same section viewed in cross-polarized light.

Table 5.2 Chemical Composition of a Petaloid Celt Found in Jamaica, Compared with Pure Jadeite from Guatemala

Oxides (%)	Celt from Jamaica	Guatemala Jadeite[a]
SiO_2	54.57	58.91
Al_2O_3	19.64	24.60
Na_2O	11.05	12.00
Fe_2O_3	5.52	1.01
CaO	4.62	1.97
MgO	2.10	1.29
TiO_2	0.49	NR
K_2O	0.26	Tr
MnO	0.13	Tr
P_2O_5	0.07	NR
Cr_2O_3	<0.01	NR
LOI	0.65	NR
Total	99.10	99.78

Note: The higher levels of Fe, Ca and Mg in the celt are due to the presence of amphibole and pyrite. NR = not reported; Tr = trace amounts

[a]Variety called Motagua Light (http://www.cigem.ca/431; accessed January 2003). Iron reported as FeO; Cr, K, and Mn are present in trace amounts only.

Figure 5.2 X-ray diffractogram for jadeite artefact (A) found in Jamaica with the international standard diffractogram for pure jadeite (B).

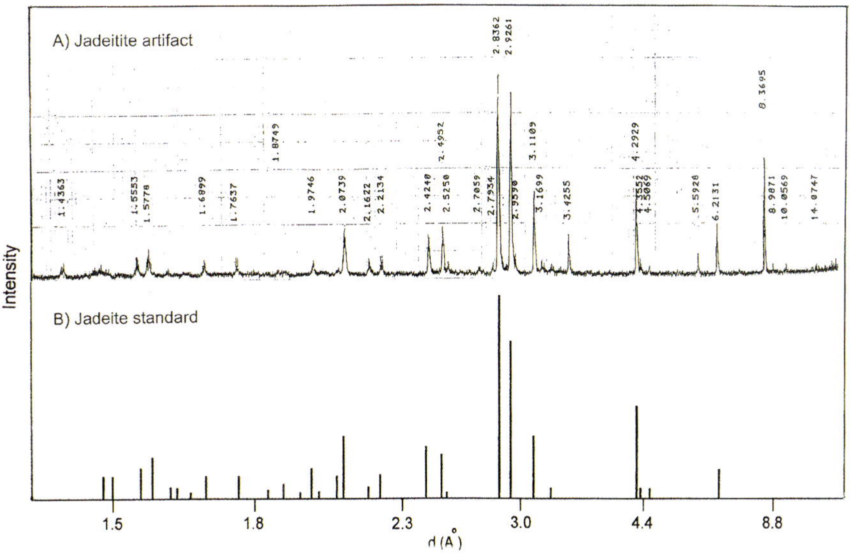

Notes:

1. Atoms in crystals are arranged in planes. The distance between each successive identical plane is denoted by the letter 'd' and is measured in angstrom units (1A° = 10^{-8} cm). When a narrow beam of X radiation of a certain wavelength (λ) is passed through a small sample of a powdered crystal, a series of beams are diffracted, or spread out, at certain angles (denoted by θ, the symbol for theta) in accordance with Bragg's Law formulated in 1913 ($n\lambda = 2d\sin\theta$). These angles and the 'd' values may be measured and recorded on a paper chart. The intensity (I) of each diffraction is represented by peaks. Since each crystalline material produces its own X-ray pattern a tabulation of θ or 'd' values with intensities is characteristic for each mineral species. The tabulated data and diffractogram may then be used for identification purposes by comparing them with data for other known substances published by the International Center for Diffraction Data.
2. Sample A was loaded into a XRD metal holder and scanned from 5° to 85° 2 theta using Co. K radiation.
3. The pattern for Sample B was re-drawn from PDF#22-1338.

XRF show that the material is soda-rich (Table 5.2), and a comparison of its XRD pattern with that of the international standard[8] proves conclusively that the pyroxene mineral is indeed jadeite (Figure 5.2). Although its origin is still somewhat obscure, it appears to have formed under metamorphic conditions and is probably more correctly termed jadeite rock or jadeitite.

JADE

To most people, jade is synonymous with the colour green. To the pre-Columbian civilizations in Central America (ancient Mesoamerica), the colour green was considered sacred and precious, just as gold was esteemed by the Spaniards and other civilizations (and is to this day). Jade was believed to possess magical properties and, as such, was considered to be the most precious object on earth.

Technically speaking, jade is a generic term that refers to two distinct minerals: nephrite and jadeite. Although superficially similar, the two are quite different in terms of their mineralogical properties. For example, jadeite is harder (H = 6.5 to 7) and denser (SG = 3.2 to 3.5) than nephrite (H = 5 to 6; SG = 3.0 to 3.1) and possesses a richer and more brilliant range of colours.

They belong to two distinct mineral groups: jadeite is a member of the Pyroxene Group and is composed of sodium aluminium silicate, expressed by the formula $NaAlSi_2O_6$, whereas nephrite is usually a mixture of two minerals of the Amphibole Group, tremolite and actinolite, composed of calcium magnesium iron silicate, expressed by the formula $Ca_2(MgFe)_5Si_8O_{22}(OH)_2$. The name jadeite is derived from the Spanish term *piedra de hijada* ("stone of the loins" or "colic stone"), while nephrite derives from the term "kidney stone", latinized to *lapis nephriticus* and eventually "nephrite".

Under a polarizing microscope pure jadeite can be seen to consist of tightly interlocking fine-grained (< =1.00mm) granular crystals of an almost mono-mineralic character and uniform texture. However, the rocks in which it is found are rarely pure and contain other pyroxene minerals often in association with albite (a plagioclase feldspar mineral). Nephrite, on the other hand, is composed of tightly interlocking fine-grained crystals that are fibrous rather than granular in character. Both, however, are tough and compact.

PRESENCE IN JAMAICA

The presence in Jamaica of material referred to as jade has been on record since the time of Sir Hans Sloane, who, in reference to "Spleen-Stone", noted:

> This Stone is opaque of a green Colour, with some pale Veins running through it very hard, and capable of a very fine Polish. . . . They are cut into thin square Pieces, and String being ty'd to Holes made in their Corners, they are fastned about the Arm. . . . This is the Piedra Hijada of the Spaniards, and Pierre de Jade of the French Authors . . .[9]

The possible presence of jade in the island was also noted by Duerden: "A metamorphic siliceous green rock resembling jade, and taking a high polish, is met with, sometimes with light and dark bands."[10] Roobol and Lee, on the other hand, did not specifically describe the existence of jadeite in Jamaica but stated: "The term 'greenstone' as used here would include the hydrous silicate mineral nephrite which is the most common variety of jade."[11] On the basis of this statement, it is clear that no attempt was made to subdivide greenstones, and it seems safe to conclude that they did not single out any celts as being composed of jadeite.

Although Jamaica has a type of metamorphic terrane (blueschist facies) with which jadeitite bodies are typically associated, no known source has yet been found. Cuba and the Dominican Republic also have exposures of metamorphic rocks (blueschist and eclogites) that could possibly contain jadeite or jadeitite, but, as in Jamaica, none has yet been discovered, although this does not mean that they do not exist.

SOURCE OF JADEITE

The story of jadeite in Mesoamerica, which comprises central and southern Mexico, Guatemala, Belize and western Honduras (Figure 5.3), begins with the earliest civilizations, namely the Olmec. The rise in the use of greenstones over darker stones such as basalt appears to be closely linked to the evolution of the Olmec serpent cult.[12] The material worked by the Olmec was long believed to have come from somewhere in Central America, most probably Mexico or Guatemala. But it was not until the mid-1950s that jadeite similar to that worked by the Olmec was found in the Motagua River Valley in Guatemala.[13]

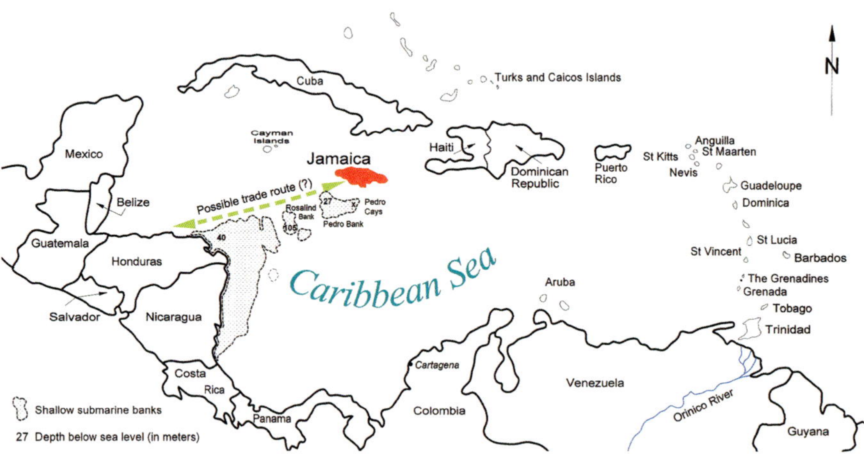

Figure 5.3 Location of Jamaica relative to Central America.

On the basis of mineralogical and chemical investigations, several varieties of jadeite from this region are now recognized, such as Motagua Light, Maya Green, Motagua Dark, Omphacite and others. It is also a matter of record that a black variety of jadeite from Guatemala was used by these early civilizations to make celts and other artefacts. This is composed largely of fine-grained chloromelanite – a greenish-black iron-bearing variety of jadeite that resembles basalt. It is highly likely that celts composed of this material are also present in Jamaica, having been imported by the Tainos, but which up to now have merely been identified as blackstone.

CONCLUSIONS AND RECOMMENDATIONS FOR FUTURE STUDIES

At present, not much is known about the possible interaction of the Tainos and the indigenous peoples of Central America, but the presence of certain finely carved geometric zoomorphic patterns on objects and fragments of pottery found on Jamaica's south coast, especially around Great Bay, St Elizabeth, suggests that these particular pieces might not have been made in Jamaica. Unfortunately, it is not an easy task to identify the exact source of clay that was used in the manufacture of such objects. Neither is it easy to determine the source provenance of jadeitite objects, with the possible exception of the very distinctive Olmec Blue material from Guatemala. But, to quote an old cliché, "Nothing ventured, nothing gained." It is my opinion that a more comprehensive investigation of the greenstone and blackstone celts found in Jamaica may yield valuable information which could contribute significantly to a better understanding of possible trading and migration patterns that, in all likelihood, occurred between the indigenous people of Jamaica and the pre-Columbian civilizations of Central America.

The amount of information that can be obtained by destructive testing techniques (such as the study of thin sections) far exceeds that which can be obtained by non-destructive methods. However, in the case of intact artefacts, it is clearly more desirable not to deface a valued object. One device that has reportedly been used with some success in differentiating true jadeite from other jade-like artefacts is a Portable Instantaneous Display and Analyzing Spectrometer, called PIDAS.[14] A more recent development has been the attachment of a Gobel Mirror on a D5000 Siemens diffractometer, the results from which seem to indicate that it may be possible to obtain X-ray powder patterns of "green stone axes" and, from the reflections obtained, determine their mineralogical composition.[15] For practical purposes, the simplest and cheapest test is to place the object in a fluid medium – usually methylene iodide – of known specific gravity (SG) and observe what happens. If the SG of the fluid is 3.1, pure jadeite will sink, nephrite (with an SG of 3.0 or 3.1) will be suspended, and jade-like minerals, such as chrysoprase and serpentine (with an SG of 2.8 or less), will float. It should be stressed, however, that while this is a rapid means of determination, especially if one is prospecting in a remote region of the world, it is not conclusive, and further test work should be undertaken.

6

Star of David Bricks

It is the opinion of this committee, that it be recommended to the house, that a small battery be built, on that part of Salt-Pond-Hill, called Drudge's Folly, to guard the path leading round the hill, by Hanson's Pond, to Port-Henderson.[1]

Overlooking the entrance to Kingston Harbour, on the southern side of Port Henderson Hill, are the remains of a small fort. According to the historical records, during the 1740s renewed hostilities between Britain and other European powers led to the erection of fortifications at Apostles' Battery, Fort Augusta (see chapter 4) and Polygon Battery at Port Royal. Then, "in martial law, 1782, . . . [the governor] for the defence and protection of this island, thought proper to order a fort to be erected . . . called Fort-Small, which commands all the southern channel coming into Port Royal Harbour".[2] It was built on a tract of land then owned by Robert Brereton, and by November 1783 the fort was almost complete and contained six mounted 12-pounder guns. In 1799, Fort Small became known as Fort Clarence (Plate 6.1) in honour of William, Duke of Clarence, who served as a naval officer in the West Indies and later became king of England.

In the late 1960s a small group of devoted historians, led by George Lechler, made their way up the hill along an overgrown path towards the site of this fort. About halfway up the hill they found some unusual grey bricks, each with a six-pointed star imprinted on one side, lying face down in the ground. This geometric pattern, composed of two overlaid equilateral triangles, has ancient origins and has served as both a mystical symbol and as a decoration. During the Middle Ages (the period in western European history extending from AD 400 to 1500), the symbol was variously referred to as the mogen David, Star of David or Shield of David, and appeared particularly among Jews. After the seventeenth century, it became the official seal of Jewish communities and a general symbol of Judaism.

Plate 6.1 Fort Clarence at the entrance to Kingston Harbour. Reproduced from the 1804 map "Couny of Middlesex, Island of Jamaica", by James Robertson. Courtesy National Library of Jamaica.

BRIEF DESCRIPTION

Externally, these bricks may be readily distinguished by their dark grey colour, metallic lustre, smooth impermeable surface and prominent Star of David symbol (Plate 6.2), which is moulded into a recessed, rectangular area on one side.[3] Within this sign is what appears to be the letter W, the significance of which is not yet clear, although one possibility is the maker's initial. On the opposite side, deeply grooved lines divide the surface of the brick into four rectangular quadrants with beveled (sloping) edges (Plate 6.3). Clearly, these are not normal bricks. They are, in fact, unique engineering bricks. They measure 8.5 × 4.25 × 3.0 inches (21.5 × 10.7 × 7.5 centimetres) and weigh, on average, 8 pounds 2.5 ounces (3.70 kilograms) with a specific gravity of 2.33. By contrast, the common yellow-brown stock bricks from London, England, that were shipped over as ballast and then used in the construction of many buildings and walls around Jamaica are porous, measure 9.0 × 4.25 × 2.5 inches (22.7 × 10.7 × 5.6 centimetres), weigh about 5 pounds (2.26 kilograms) and have a specific gravity of 2.13.

Plate 6.2 Star of David brick with the letter W.

Internally, the fabric consists of some small (up to 5 millimetres in length) but prominent cream-coloured, rounded to sub-rounded fragments of hardened clay, together with dark angular particles, many fine cracks and small circular (about 1 millimetre in diameter) vesicles, or holes, embedded in a reddish-tinged sandy-textured matrix (Plate 6.4). These bricks must have been made by compressing impure clay into specially made moulds that were lightly smeared with a colouring agent and then firing at a very high temperature – probably about 2,200°F (1,200°C).

Plate 6.3 Other side of brick with four rectangular quadrants and bevelled edges.

Plate 6.4 Cross-section showing the interior of the brick.

COMPOSITION

A preliminary semi-quantitative analysis of two brick fragments, carried out independently at Alcan Jamaica Company, Kirkvine, Jamaica, and SGS Services, Toronto, Canada, by X-ray fluorescence spectrometry (XRF), shows that the brick is composed largely of the oxides of silicon, aluminium and iron, as shown in Table 6.1. For purposes of comparison, two other bricks were examined by the same technique – one was from the ruins of Colbeck Castle, St Catherine, and the other from Seville, St Ann. There is a close chemical correlation between the Star of David and the Colbeck Castle bricks, which suggests – but does not yet prove – that the clay might have come from the same source. But we should be careful not to speculate further until a more complete elemental analysis has been carried out. On the other hand, the results clearly show that the material used by the Spanish for making bricks in the early 1500s was much richer in lime (CaO) and significantly lower in silica (SiO_2), aluminium (Al_2O_3) and iron (Fe_2O_3).

Although further work needs to be undertaken to explain the metallic lustre, a preliminary chemical analysis of thirty-four elements both on the surface and at the centre of one of the bricks reveals that, with the exception of zinc (Zn), there is not much difference. At surface the content of this element is 288 parts per million, and in the centre it is 103 parts per million. This suggests the presence of a zinc glaze.

PURPOSE

Why, one wonders, would anyone go to the trouble of making such elaborate bricks? To the best of my knowledge, no authoritative letters, reports or other written documents have yet been found explaining exactly who made these bricks. And up until May 2003, no one with whom I spoke seemed to know why they were made. So it is left to historians and others to apply deductive reasoning. This may have been the technique adapted in 1998 by Mrs Jacky Shepard, the writer of a one-page pamphlet that accompanies small silver jewellery replicas of these bricks distributed by Swiss Stores of Kingston, Jamaica.[4]

According to this source, when the British captured Jamaica there was a Portuguese bricklayer by the name of Guitterez living at St Jago de la Vega (now known as Spanish Town). It is said that he was a "crypto-Jew" or "Marana" who practised "his religion in secret while pretending to be of another faith". Because of his skill he was employed to make "gunnery bricks" using a special variety of "dense clay" from the Spanish Town area. His bricks facilitated the transport of heavy gun carriages and cannons, which the British used to defend their fortifications. "As a rebellious, deeply religious Jew, Guitterez defiantly immortalized his religion by moulding the Star of David into each brick" and placed this closest to the soil. These bricks, the pamphlet states, "lay quietly at Fort Augusta for centuries, known only to fishermen until members of the United Congregation of Israelites discovered them in the early 1970s". The pamphlet, however, makes no mention of the bricks found on the flank of the hill leading up to the site of Fort Small, at an altitude of about 180 feet (56 metres) above sea level.

Another puzzling aspect of these mysterious bricks is their origin. According to the pamphlet, Guitterez "came to Jamaica prior to the British capture of the island in 1655". But if this is true, he could hardly have been alive

Table 6.1 Chemical Comparison of Star of David Bricks with Other Bricks

Oxides (%)	Star of David, Fort Clarence[a]	Star of David, Fort Clarence[b]	Colbeck Castle, St Catherine[a]	Seville Estate, St Ann[b]
SiO_2	59.54	63.81	60.43	23.66
Al_2O_3	20.68	20.17	18.03	11.31
Fe_2O_3	11.55	9.94	12.25	4.90
Na_2O	0.64	0.54	nd	nd
CaO	0.94	0.44	2.98	57.01
K_2O	2.52	2.24	2.09	0.77
MgO	1.43	1.27	2.31	1.41
TiO_2	1.06	0.99	1.18	0.49
MnO	0.11	0.11	0.19	0.05
P_2O_5	0.09	0.10	0.08	ND
Cr_2O_3	0.01	<0.01	<0.01	0.01
ZnO	0.02	nd	0.02	0.02
ZrO_2	0.03	nd	0.03	0.04
V_2O_5	0.02	nd	0.02	ND
Other	1.35	0.39	0.39	0.33
% Total	100.00	100.00	100.00	100.00

Source: After A.R.D. Porter, "The Unique Star of David Bricks", *Jamaican Historical Society Bulletin* 11, nos. 11 and 12 (2003): 345–50.
nd = not determined; ND = not detected.
[a]XRF analyses by Alcan Jamaica Company, Kirkvine.
[b]XRF analysis by SGS, Toronto, Canada, on a duplicate sample.

ninety years later, when Fort Augusta was under construction. On the other hand, it is conceivable that he could have made and stockpiled the bricks somewhere safe before his death, or passed on his skill to someone else. Alternatively, it has been suggested that the bricks might have been brought to Jamaica as ballast stones on sailing ships and then used in the construction of certain forts. Although this remains a possibility, it seems highly unlikely, as no such ballast bricks have yet been found anywhere else.

Clearly, further fieldwork had to be undertaken to try to find answers to at least some of the many puzzling questions. In this regard, Evelyn Thompson of the Jamaica National Heritage Trust and I visited Fort Augusta in April 2003, but were unable to find any visible evidence that these bricks were ever used either in the original construction or to effect repairs. Our next objective was to visit the old Fort Small site and present-day Fort Clarence. To get there, however, was more complex than Lechler's earlier visit, as the parochial road from Braeton to the ruined fortification on the southern side of the hill had been blocked off sometime in the 1970s. As a consequence, we decided to approach it by sea. Thus, on the morning of Tuesday, 13 May 2003, a small group – George Lechler, Kristina Porter, Evelyn Thompson and Ricardo Tyndall from the Jamaica National Heritage Trust, and I – crossed the harbour in a small boat. The trip was made possible with the help of Dr Mona Webber from the Department of Life Sciences at the University of the West Indies, who kindly arranged for the group to use a departmental outboard motorboat stationed at the Port Royal Marine Laboratory. On our way up the cactus-lined road leading to the top of the hill, a few loose, broken Star of David bricks were found in the bushes, and some unbroken bricks in mint condition, together with ordinary red bricks, were seen on the road surface. Near the top are the remains of an early reinforced concrete structure. Incredibly, the floor of one of the rooms remains essentially intact, with the bricks installed in a diagonal pattern and the Star of David placed face down. Presumably this building was erected sometime between 1907 (when reinforced concrete was introduced into Jamaica) and the beginning of World War I in 1914. It appears that this was a switch room for the power generators. Although there is no evidence to suggest that any of the other rooms were floored with these bricks, numerous broken ones were lying scattered around on the ground at the back of the building. On the basis of this remarkable find, it appears that these bricks may not be as old as previously suspected, but the intrigue surrounding who made them, when and where still remains. Although we may never know the full story behind the origin of these unique bricks, it is possible that the British War Records Office in London may be able to throw further light on this fascinating subject.

7

Other Stone Artefacts and Objects

Artefacts include any objects used or made by human beings. Although many of those found in Jamaica have been mentioned in a number of different publications, there are still a few objects about which little information exists, and which warrant further description and illustration. These include beads, boiler-house stones, date stones and inscription stones, dripstones, gunflints, metates, mealing stones and manos, spherical stones, stone mortars, and whetstones.

BEADS

Small cylindrical beads, up to 1 inch (2.54 centimetres) in diameter, perforated by a central hole, have been found at several Taino occupation sites in Jamaica (Plate 7.1). In a study undertaken in the mid-1970s it was reported that eight specimens from four different sites were all "composed of white chalcedony containing small green crystals of the minerals epidote and chlorite", and the authors concluded that they could have originated from the greenstone belt of the southern Blue Mountains Inlier.[1] Since then a large number of broken beads have been found at a site in southern Clarendon, suggesting that this might have been a manufactur-

Plate 7.1 Ornamental bead with central hole from a Taino site in Clarendon. It measures 14 millimetres by 10 millimetres and consists chiefly of chalcedony (white) with lesser amounts of green epidote and chlorite.

ing centre for such beads. In 1990 similar material was also unearthed at a newly discovered Taino site at Chancery Hall, in upper St Andrew.[2] Narrow silica-rich cylindrical pendants, measuring up to 3 inches (7.5 centimetres) in length and perforated at one end by a hole, have also been uncovered at some Taino sites. While it is geologically possible that the parent material for all of these objects originated in Jamaica, it is still not known with certainty what abrasive materials the Tainos used to rub them down to attain the desired shape and size. Unless they brought emery rock or some other very hard abrasive material from elsewhere, they would have had to use local quartz-rich substances such as chert, flint and sandstone and various volcanic rocks. Spherical beads composed of white limestone have also been found at some sites, but this material is much softer and more easily worked than either chalcedony or quartz.

BOILER-HOUSE STONES

In 1985 the *Geological Society of Jamaica Newsletter* carried a brief article about some pebbles with opal-like physical properties being found along the coastline east of Montego Bay.[3] Later that year, I set off in search of this mysterious material and luckily was able to find a few on the beach not far from the ruins of the Rose Hall sugar factory. The pebbles have a rounded surface (a result of rolling in the surf), and contain numerous small spherical pores, the walls of which are smooth and unlined (Plate 7.2). Their colour varies from milky white or pale aquamarine to blue or green, but some have an amber-like to dark smoky tint. Freshly fractured surfaces are conchoidal and vitreous (glassy), with no evidence of any crystalline morphology.

With the aid of a polarizing microscope and an X-ray diffractometer, the specimens are seen to consist largely of an amorphous phase with a small amount of microcrystalline material. No opaline silica was detected. The refractive index (RI) of these pebbles ranges from 1.51 to 1.53, and energy dispersive X-ray methods show that silicon and oxygen are the principal elements. Also present are several other elements that give rise to the elevated RI compared with that of pure fused quartz (RI = 1.46) and opal (RI = 1.43–1.45). The chemical composition of one pebble, analysed at an Alcan laboratory in Quebec, Canada, by XRF, is shown in Table 7.1. On the basis of this investigation, it has been concluded that these specimens are not opal or fused glass, but rather impure silica glass.

Plate 7.2 Boiler-house stones from Rose Hall estate, St James.

How did calcium-rich silica glass pebbles find their way to the coast? Could their proximity to the sugar factory be a clue – and, if so, what was the connection? In search of answers to these questions, I sought out the views of some of Jamaica's older and more knowledgeable sugar experts, one of whom showed me a large piece that he had obtained from the Bernard Lodge sugar factory several years

Table 7.1 Chemical Composition of a Boiler-House Stone from Rose Hall Estate, St James

Constituents as Oxides*	Percentage (%)
SiO_2	65.50
CaO	15.52
K_2O	6.49
Al_2O_3	2.80
MgO	2.67
Na_2O	2.50
P_2O_5	1.95
Fe_2O_3	0.90
TiO_2	0.20
MnO	0.03
ZrO_2	0.01
SO_3	<0.10
Cr_2O_3	<0.01
V_2O_5	<0.01
ZnO	<0.01
Ga_2O_3	<0.01
Loss of mass	0.41

Note: XRF analysis carried out at the Alcan Research and Development Centre, Quebec, Canada.

ago. "They were lying on the ground outside the boiler house," he said.

Many years ago life on the sugar estate was very different from the way it is today. For a long time the cane cutter and hand loader were paid on the basis of cane weight. To increase his take, he placed stones in the middle of the cart. The cane load then passed through the crushing mills (or rollers). The squeezed cane stalk (also referred to as "trash" or bagasse), together with the crushed stones and chopped firewood, was then fed into the furnace to be used as fuel. The temperatures in these furnaces varied from 1,500°F to 1,800°F (800°C to 980°C), and it was the fusion of the calcium-rich stones with the silica-rich inorganic residue that combined to form the slag referred to as boiler-house stones.

DATE STONES AND INSCRIPTION STONES

In 1688, when Hans Sloane visited the Seville estate at St Ann's Bay, he observed the remains of a stone church, the construction of which had begun in 1524. Over the door was a Latin inscription, the approximate English translation of which follows.

> Peter Martyr of Angleria, an Italian,
> citizen of Milan, chief missionary
> and Abbot of this island, a member of
> the council of the Indies, first raised this
> building from its foundation with bricks
> and squared stone; formerly it was built
> of wood and twice destroyed by fire.[4]

By chance a part of the dedication stone, bearing a portion of the Latin inscription recorded by Sloane, was found sometime between 1950 and 1951. It was embedded in the wall of the old English fort, then being used as a slaughterhouse, at St Ann's Bay.[5] The fort had been constructed with materials obtained from the Spanish ruins at Sevilla Nueva (or New Seville, as it was then called). The engraved segment of stone was retrieved by the Institute of Jamaica and (at the time of writing) is still on display at the Seville Heritage Park Museum.

In 1967, another engraved stone of historical importance was found. On this occasion an expeditionary team, led by Alan Teulon, to the upper reaches of the Stoney River Valley in Portland discovered a large stone at the site of Nanny Town on the banks of the river, which bears the following inscription:

Decem 17 1734
This town was took
By Coll Brook
And after kept
By Capt Cooke
Till July 1735[6]

This etching was done to commemorate the fall of Nanny Town to the militia under Colonel Brook. Thereafter, it was guarded by British troops almost continuously until the peace treaty with the Maroons in 1739. In 1973, a United Kingdom–based organization, the Scientific Exploration Society, in conjunction with the Jamaican government, carried out further exploration, and I was privileged to be part of the team.

During the 1740s and the second half of the eighteenth century, numerous estate houses, sugar works, aqueducts, bridges and other structures were erected. Most, if not all, bore the stamp of the year that construction either commenced or was completed. In the case of buildings, the inscribed stone – hereafter referred to as a date stone – was usually placed over the arch of the main entrance, or the date was etched into the keystone, which was then embedded in the fabric of the arch. One of the earliest stones, with the date 1745, can still be seen over the back entrance to the Seville Great House, but because an annex was added later, the date stone is now within the main building and thus protected from the elements.

The following are some other surviving structures with important dates and inscriptions. At the Good Hope estate in Trelawny, a stone tablet on the wall of a small building behind the Great House known as the Ice House records the dates when the estate was settled and the house begun. It reads:

Thomas Williams
Jun. From the Parish
of Westmoreland
began Settle this
estate April y 7th
1744 and Nam'd
it Good Hope
this House Built
in 1755

Plate 7.3 Bath stone at Fort Augusta, inscribed with the year of emplacement, 1760, and various initials.

A few years later, work had commenced on the construction of a brick and stone aqueduct on the Hope property and a sugar mill on the Mona estate, in Kingston. Despite the onslaught of natural disasters and the ravages of man in the name of development, both structures still stand – the former with its metal plaque dated 1758, and the latter with the date 1759 clearly etched into one of the keystones of local white limestone (see Plate 2.3). At the same time, the construction of Fort Augusta at the western end of Kingston Harbour was well advanced. Although no official date stone has yet been found, some of the large rectangular honey-coloured oolitic limestone blocks imported from Bath for use in the construction of the central bastion are initialled, and the date 1760 is clearly etched on one of them (Plate 7.3).

Towards the end of the eighteenth century two other interesting buildings were erected. The slightly earlier structure, a slave hospital of finely dressed local white limestone, was constructed on the Orange Valley estate in western Trelawny. Today the building is roofless, but on the inner wall over the front entrance is a stone tablet with a Latin inscription, which states that the hospital was designed by E Earl, an architect, and built in MDCCXCVII (that is, 1797), by H.N. Jarrett.

With the expansion of the sugar industry still in full swing in Trelawny, construction of a boiler house and other buildings was about to commence at Gales Valley, situated just over 4.5 miles (7.5 kilometres) east-southeast of the Orange Valley sugar factory. In 1955, the old boiler house was donated by the owners of Hampden estate to Her Royal Highness, Princess Alice, who was then Chancellor of the University of the West Indies. She arranged for it to be dismantled, block by block, under the supervision of the late A.D. Scott. Each building stone was meticulously numbered, then transported by road to the Mona campus of the University of the West Indies and reassembled. It took three years to complete the task of reconstruction, and when it was done this beautiful Georgian building, made with finely dressed white limestone from the parish of Trelawny, was reborn as the University Chapel.[7] A close inspection of the blocks will reveal that macrofossils are rare, but smaller fossils, referred to as benthic foraminifers, are present, and on this basis these building stones have been classified as belonging to either the Bonny Gate or Montpelier formation.[8] An interesting architectural feature not highlighted in brochures is the prominent row of dentils below the eaves. And immediately below the dentils on the northern side of the chapel are the largest date stones, clearly marked 1799 (Plate 7.4).

Plate 7.4 Large limestone blocks below the row of dentils reveal the date 1799. Originally part of a sugar complex in Trelawny, the building is now the University Chapel, on the Mona campus of the University of the West Indies.

The first-class workmanship that went into the construction of eighteenth-century Jamaican great houses and their associated sugar works was also applied to many churches. Unfortunately, very few survived the harsh forces of nature, of which fire, hurricanes and earthquakes were the main destroyers. As a consequence, most of the structures standing today were extensively repaired and enlarged, or totally rebuilt. One such example is the very elegant St John's Anglican Church in Black River. This impressive building, typical of the English-style church with a tower, nave and chancel, is made of a combination of imported yellow-brown London stock bricks (which form the walls) and neatly dressed local white limestone (which form the quoins). Enclosing the churchyard is a red-brick wall capped by more than fifty large, coarse-grained granite copings, most likely imported from Cornwall in south-west England. Over the doorway in the tower at the western end of the church is the following inscription:

> The first stone of this
> CHURCH was laid on the 18
> day of July in the year of our
> LORD 1837 by the Hon ble D.
> ROBERTSON being
> Custos, the Rev d Tho. P.
> Williams Rector,
> J. MILLER & A. MOORE
> Esq., Churchwarden.
> Crawford & . . . builders.

As was the custom in many other parts of the world, the early churches of Jamaica contain many interesting and some very elaborately carved monuments, wall plaques and tombstones honouring famous people and active members of the congregation. The next time you visit a place of worship, take time to examine the history that is written in these commemorative stones and, if you are so inclined, the type of material in which the messages are engraved.

DRIPSTONES

Calcarenite is the name applied to a particular variety of limestone that is composed of small, rounded to sub-rounded, sand-sized particles of calcium carbonate loosely cemented together, giving it extreme porosity. As a consequence of this property, calcarenite rock was fashioned into receptacles, called dripstones or filtering stones, that were used to purify water. Although it has not yet been established with certainty when dripstones were first used in Jamaica, they have existed in the island since December 1687, when Sir Hans Sloane arrived in Jamaica as personal physician to Christopher Monk, the new governor. He wrote:

> The porous Stones for percolating water is the best remedy for this muddiness; they must be clean'd every day, and sometimes the water put through

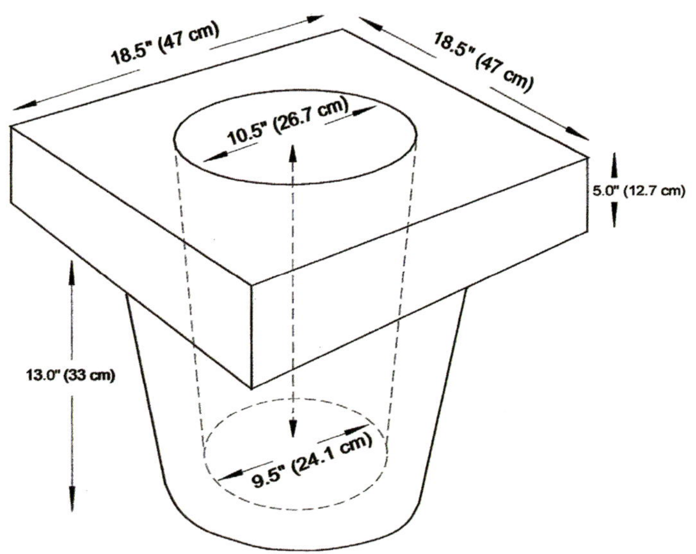

Figure 7.1 Dimensions of a typical Barbados dripstone

Table 7.2 Chemical Composition of Two Different Imported Dripstones

Oxides (%)	Barbados Dripstone[a]	Canary Island Dripstone[b]
CaO	55.15	35.44
SiO_2	0.46	16.58
Al_2O_3	0.04	4.52
Na_2O	0.04	1.29
Fe_2O_3	0.08	3.67
MgO	0.72	5.84
TiO_2	0.01	1.07
MnO	<0.01	0.11
K_2O	0.01	1.09
P_2O_5	0.08	0.24
Cr_2O_3	<0.01	0.03
LOI	43.35	30.45
TOTAL	99.94	100.33
Selected trace elements, parts per million (ppm)		
Rubidium (Rb)	12	9
Strontium (Sr)	1710	1320
Yttrium (Y)	<2	36
Zirconium (Z)	53	43
Niobium (Nb)	<2	27
Barium (Ba)	28	192

[a]Pure carbonate sand or calcarenite.
[b]Impure calcareous sandstone.

them twice or thrice. They are brought from the Canaries to the Spanish Main, and thence to Jamaica. They are made into the form of Mortars, the water being put into their Concave side, foul and troubled, passes through them, and is filtred, leaving its filth in the pores of the stone. Sometimes this water is pass'd through three of these plac'd one under another.[9]

In the mid-1750s, however, Patrick Browne, who referred to them as the "The percolating stone, or the porous sandy Cos", said that "This stone is frequently introduced here in the manufactured state;...It is a native of Madera and Barbadoes."[10] This apparent contradiction as to the stones' country of origin is easy to reconcile, as indicated in the following passage taken from a narrative written in 1774: "Antigua ... is almost destitute of fresh springs, therefore the water principally used is rain, which the inhabitants collect in some cisterns, this water, after being drawn from the reservoir is filtered through a Barbadoes stone."[11] At that time dripstone quarries included Chapel in St Phillip and the Mount Plantation in St George, but today only Chapel Quarry is in operation.[12] As noted by Fraser, "Dripstones were carved of coral stone (there used to be a thriving trade in dripstones as they were exported to neighbouring islands)",[13] and the following passage by Robertson gives corroboration:

> The statistics of imports in the Blue Books give some information. Blue Books for nine of the years 1853 to 1869 are available in the [West India Reference] Library and in those nine years 292 dripstones were brought in, mainly from other West Indian Islands, but a few were from South America. The largest number in one year was 91 in 1869. Between 1870 and 1879 only two dripstones were imported in 1874.[14]

Generally speaking, the dripstones from Barbados are creamy white in colour, have a square rim with a flat base, and are fairly uniform in size (Figure 7.1). They are carved out of Pleistocene reef material, which ranges from 240,000 to 270,000 years in age.[15] By comparison, those suspected to have originated from Tenerife in the Canary Islands have a rounded base and a speckled, salt and pepper-like appearance, owing to a mix of light- and dark-coloured minerals which makes them chemically different (see Table 7.2). They may be geologically older than those from Barbados, but this remains to be confirmed.

Calcarenite similar to that found in Barbados also occurs on a tiny, remote island in the Pacific called Norfolk Island, located 930 miles (1,500 kilometres) east of Brisbane, Australia. Dripstones were manufactured from it as well, but according to the records this activity did not commence until 1825 or shortly thereafter.[16] A recent publication by Ronald Coleman, a retired marine archaeologist from Queensland, Australia, traces the origin of dripstones and points out that they were also widely used on ships at sea.[17] It is quite possible, therefore, that a few Norfolk dripstones found their way to Jamaica via a circuitous route, but further research into the origin and provenance of dripstones will have to be undertaken.

Dripstones in Jamaica were most commonly housed in a portable tapered wooden lattice structure (about 4 feet or 1.2 metres high), at the base of which a jar was placed to collect the filtered water. In some affluent homes dripstones were located in a specially designed recess in a wall or behind a staircase (see Plate 2.7). With the coming of treated piped water to many communities throughout Jamaica and other Caribbean islands, the need for filtering eventually became obsolete, but that did not signal the total abandonment of these imported objects, as many homeowners used them as flowerpots (both indoors and outdoors), and this practice is still evident in many parts of Jamaica today.

GUNFLINTS

Several centuries ago rifles, pistols, muskets and wall guns could not be fired without the use of small pieces of wedge-shaped flint. When the trigger was pulled, the sharp edge of the flint struck a metal plate (in the section known as flintlock), which produced the sparks that ignited the gunpowder and fired the shots.

Plate 7.5 British gunflints found near Martello Tower, St Andrew.

Flintlocks were introduced into the English army about 1666 and were in general use at the beginning of the eighteenth century.[18] Gunflints fashioned in France were produced mainly from a yellowish- to honey-coloured chert. British gunflints, on the other hand, were crafted (by a process called knapping) from a dark-grey to black flint (Plate 7.5) that occurs largely as nodules embedded in white chalky limestone in the vicinity of Brandon, on the border of Norfolk and Suffolk counties, in southeast England. Initially, the flint was knapped to produce one firing edge, but around 1780 the French invention of a double-edged flint gun reached the town. Just before the Battle of Waterloo, fought on 18 June 1815 at Waterloo, a small town near Brussels, all gunflints for the British Army were ordered from Brandon. The following year the order was nil, and by 1835 gunflints in England were superseded by percussion caps. In Jamaica, large quantities were imported for the use of the militia in the seventeenth and eighteenth centuries. In 1701, for example, it was reported that 5,000 flints, at a cost of 10 shillings per 1,000, were to be sent to the island;[19] by contrast, in 1816 more than 70,000 flints (49,237 for muskets and 23,343 for pistols) belonged to the island of Jamaica, in the charge of the island storekeeper in Spanish Town.[20] Specimens of such gunflints, varying from about 1 to 2 inches (2.5 to 5 centimetres) square and dating back to this period, can still be found lying on the surface or in the topsoil at some of the island's old fortifications.

METATES, MEALING STONES AND MANOS

Plate 7.6 A three-legged metate carved out of granitic rock. It was most likely imported from Central America.

As previously mentioned, the Tainos used stone axes as a tool to clear land, make canoes and carve other wooden objects, but what did they use to prepare food? Among the objects that have been found in Jamaica at known midden sites are some large, fairly heavy stone blocks with a shallow concave surface, as well as some smooth flattened slabs of stone. In an account of the aboriginal remains in Jamaica, Duerden refers to these objects as parts of "mealing stones"; he also describes "three-legged" and "tripod metates", one of which was "carved out of a single block of dolerite".[21] Since then, judging by the paucity of published data, such objects apparently have generated little interest locally. In parts of Central America and the southwestern United States, the native peoples used similar stone objects for grinding corn (maize), seeds, nuts and other food items. These ancient food processors, or metates, were quite elaborate, being made in the form of flat, slanted stone slabs or curved slabs supported by three legs (Plate 7.6). The objects referred to by Duerden can be seen in the collection of the Institute of Jamaica, but it seems to me, based on a brief examination of these and others in private collections, that the three-legged metates were fashioned elsewhere, probably Central and/or South America, and imported into Jamaica in the finished state. But a more detailed study, similar to that described in chapter 5, needs to be undertaken.

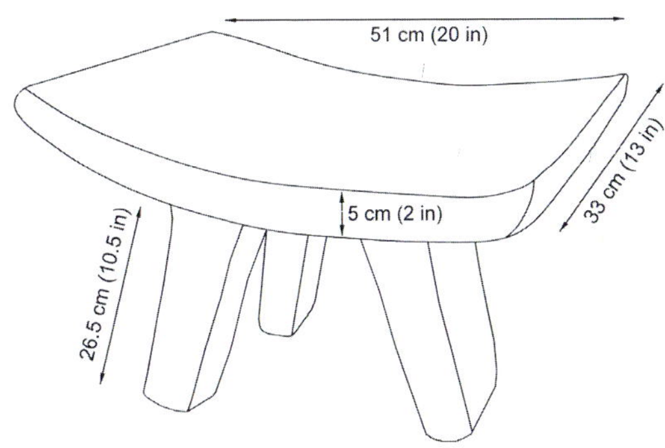

Figure 7.2 Dimensions of a three-legged granitic metate found in Jamaica.

A significantly large number of stone blocks and slabs with concave surfaces have been found on the crest of a hill just east of Harbour View, at Tower Hill, and on Long Mountain. Most of these are composed of volcanic igneous rocks, such as keratophyre and andesite, similar to material that occurs in eastern St Andrew and western St Thomas.[22] These local stone blocks are quite heavy, and in some places they were carried by the Tainos to their village sites several hundred feet uphill, where they were used as mealing stones.

Duerden also reported the presence of "rollers, evidently intended for use with metates".[23] Such objects were held in the hand and rolled back and forth over the metate to grate the food. They varied from short oval or cylindrical bars to long spindle-shaped rolling pins. They are referred to as handstones, mullers or manos (Spanish for "hands"). According to Duerden, "they are mostly formed of some doleritic rock". Although no serious study of these implements has yet been undertaken, I have seen only one, very symmetrical, oval-shaped mano, fashioned out of white limestone. It was found in a topographically enclosed limestone valley in the parish of St Ann, along with a large concave mealing stone made out of volcanic rock, similar to material in eastern Jamaica. Clearly, the latter was transported a long way, but when and by whom will probably never be known, as neither was recovered from any mapped Taino site.

SPHERICAL STONES

Small, spherical, creamy white to beige-coloured stones or pebble-like objects, ranging in size from a marble (0.4 inches or 1 centimetre) up to a billiard ball (about 1.8 inches or 4.5 centimetres) have been found at various sites in St Andrew, St Catherine, Portland and other parishes. At first glance they resemble stones that have been rounded and polished by abrasion and washed up along the shoreline. Perhaps some of them were rounded naturally, but several that have been found at inland Taino sites, far removed from riverbeds and coastal gravel deposits, appear to be stony masses reminiscent of gastroliths (colloquially called gizzard stones). Since birds do not have teeth, they swallow small stones to help grind up hard-to-assimilate food, and over time these become more rounded and polished within the gizzard. Stomach stones are also associated with some reptiles.

A preliminary examination of several of these objects reveals that some of them effervesce instantaneously in a solution of dilute hydrochloric acid. In addition, they are soft and easily scratched by a knife blade. This type is composed of limestone. Another variety is hard and cannot be scratched by a knife blade. It bears a strong resemblance to dense chert. But some have a lower specific gravity (SG = 2.1–2.2) and hardness (H = 5.5–6.5) than chert (SG = 2.6, H = 7) and may consist of amorphous silica (in the form of common opal), possibly with small amounts of finely disseminated clay, while others appear to be made from bone.

Plate 7.7 Mortars carved out of stone are a reminder of past industries and lifestyles. Fashioned out of local limestone, the small mortar on the left was used for medicinal purposes, while the one in the centre was probably used to grind corn and other foodstuffs. The mortar at right, measuring 12 inches (30 centimetres) across, is carved out of marble and was imported in the eighteenth or nineteenth century.

The fact that some of these small rounded objects have been found at Taino sites raises the question of whether any of them played a utilitarian role during the Tainos' occupation of Jamaica. We may never know for certain, but a more detailed investigation similar to that undertaken for the boiler-house stones may throw further light on the subject.

STONE MORTARS

In many civilizations mortars and pestles were used to grind and mix plant material to make assorted pastes, powders, poultices and ointments for medicinal purposes. They were also used to prepare food products. A variety of stone mortars have been found in Jamaica, ranging from small, shallow, cup-like bowls to very large, deep, frequently tapered containers. Most are simple in design and roughly fashioned out of Jamaican white limestone (Plate 7.7). Although no attempt has yet been undertaken to study them in any detail, it is believed that some were made by people of African descent to prepare *fufu*, a staple food item in Ghana and elsewhere, made by pounding yam, or a mixture of cassava and plantain, with a long wooden pestle in a stone mortar until it glutinized into a ball, free of lumps. Stone mortars were also used in Jamaica to pulverize corn. But the white marble mortars with the characteristic tapering cylindrical shape and four equally spaced lugs around the outer rim were imported and are either eighteenth or nineteenth century in age. These items were a feature in many plantation homes and probably served more than one purpose. For example, an interesting photograph in *Treasures of Barbados* shows that this type of mortar also functioned as a receptacle beneath dripstones to catch filtered water.[24]

WHETSTONES

Stones that are hard, abrasive and suitable for sharpening implements are referred to as whetstones. They are usually fine-grained and siliceous, such as emery rock, sandstone, quartzite and novaculite, but where these are not available other rock types and abrasive sand can be, and have been, used for this purpose. In recent years, I have examined a number of superb specimens of Jamaican rocks with prominent groove marks that were clearly used as whetstones, and several have been found at Tower Hill on Dallas Mountain (St Andrew) and in the vicinity of Harbour View, extending eastwards towards Bull Bay.[25] As noted earlier, many mealing stones have also been found in this region, which strongly suggests that this region might have been a domestic lithic centre – that is, an area where petaloid celts and other stone implements were fashioned before being traded.

Appendix

Some Significant Events in the History of Jamaica

Period of occupation: 650–1508 (858 years)
Colonizers: Pre-Columbian inhabitants

650 Tainos arrived in Jamaica via migration through the Antilles and Hispaniola from the Orinoco basin.

1494 Christopher Columbus arrived in Jamaica on his second West Indian voyage, carrying sugar cane, which he planted on the northern coast of Hispaniola.

1508 The first Spanish settlers arrived in Jamaica.

1509–1655 (146 years)
Colonizer: Spain

1509 Spain colonized Jamaica; Juan de Esquivel was appointed governor by Diego Columbus.

1510 Construction of Sevilla la Nueva commenced.

1513 The first Africans arrived in Jamaica.

1515 Sugar cane was brought to Jamaica by Garay from Hispaniola.

1524 Peter Martyr began work on the first Spanish-built stone church, on Seville estate in St Ann's Bay.

1526 With Martyr's death, emphasis was placed on repairing the fort.

1533 Seville was essentially abandoned, and work on the church ceased.

1534 Villa de la Vega (now known as Spanish Town) was established as the new capital.

1655–1962 (307 years)
Colonizer: Britain

1655 The British captured Jamaica. Spanish Town remained the capital city, but Port Royal gained prominence and construction of fortifications commenced.

1658 Yassi, a Spanish guerilla, was defeated at Rio Nuevo.

1664 Henry Morgan moved to Port Royal. Construction began on St. Andrew Parish Church.

1665 Fort Cromwell was enlarged, restored and renamed Fort Charles. Although partly damaged in 1692, it was subsequently repaired and remodelled. It remains the oldest surviving monument of the British occupation of Port Royal and Jamaica.

1671 St Peter's Church, The Alley, was completed. The church was destroyed in the 1692 earthquake and rebuilt at least twice between then and 1735.

1684 The 80-ton *Lambe of Bristol* arrived at Port Royal with twenty grindstones in its cargo.

1687 Sir Hans Sloane arrived in Jamaica. He wrote two books and collected many samples.

1692 An earthquake destroyed Port Royal, then Jamaica's chief city, including its brick houses, which comprised about half of Port Royal's estimated two thousand houses. The rest were built of wood.

1693 Construction of Kingston commenced in an area covered by trees and grass.

1703 Port Royal was razed by a terrible fire that reduced most of the houses to ashes.

1703–13 War of the Spanish Succession; Jamaica became a regular naval station for the British Navy, with Port Royal being the base.

1714 The majestic new cathedral in Spanish Town, built of red bricks and featuring coloured stained-glass windows, was completed. Inside the church are many superb marble monuments sculpted by John Bacon and others. The tower was added in 1817.

1722 Port Royal was almost demolished again, this time by a violent hurricane on 28 August.

1726 St Peter's Anglican Church at Port Royal was completed. It replaced the original church, which sank in 1692. The blue-grey and white floor tiles are original.

1728 Coffee was introduced and barbecues (paved terraces) constructed to dry the beans. Barbecues were also used to dry pimento, annatto and bissy (kola nuts from Africa).

1734 Nanny Town was taken by the British militia. A carved stone dated 1734 was found at the site in 1967.

1742 Construction of the hospital at Port Royal was in progress, and Admiral Vernon recorded that the unloading of fifty thousand bricks from the last stoneships had begun. The hospital was completed and in use by 1743, but it was ruined in 1771, 1787 and 1812.

1774 Edward Long published the two-volume *History of Jamaica*.

1782 Nanny Town was attacked and destroyed.

1790 The 8-foot statue of Rodney, sculpted by John Bacon in white Italian marble, arrived in Jamaica. It is located in the Rodney Memorial in Spanish Town Square.

1793 Breadfruit was brought to Jamaica from Tahiti by Captain William Bligh.

1801 An iron bridge was erected over the Rio Cobre at Spanish Town.

1807 The slave trade between Africa and Jamaica was abolished by the British Parliament.

1815 The first true geological map of anywhere in the world was produced in England by William Smith. This gave rise to stratigraphy and expanded the science of geology.

1817 Construction began on the cast iron naval hospital at Port Royal.

1827 The first geological account of Jamaica and the first geological map, of the eastern part of the island, were published by Henry de la Beche in England.

1834 Slavery was abolished throughout the British Empire. The first issue of the *Gleaner* was published.

1838 Emancipation Day occurrred on 1 August.

1842 The first East Indian immigrants arrived from India.

1845 Railway service commenced in Jamaica, between Kingston and Angels.

1851 A cholera epidemic swept across Jamaica, claiming thirty thousand lives.

1853 A lighthouse was erected at Plumb Point on the Palisadoes.

1854 The first Chinese arrived in Jamaica aboard the SS *Epsom*.

1858 The first Jamaican postage stamps were issued.

1865 Slaves rose up against their masters in the Morant Bay Rebellion. Paul Bogle and George W. Gordon were executed.

1869 James G. Sawkins et al. published *Reports on the Geology of Jamaica*.

1872 The seat of government was transferred to Kingston from Spanish Town.

1874 Tea was introduced to Jamaica from Ceylon.

1879 The Institute of Jamaica was founded.

1882–85 Railway lines were completed from Old Harbour to Porus and from Spanish Town to Ewarton via Bog Walk.

1888 The Royal Artillery Store (aka the Giddy House) at Port Royal was built.

1891 Kingston played host to the Great International Exhibition. Five new hotels were built. The Lands Department was formed to facilitate the sale of government land to small farmers.

1894 The railway line from Porus to Montego Bay via Catadupa was completed.

1905 The naval station closed down, and the British Navy withdrew from Port Royal.

1907 Earthquake and fire destroyed much of Kingston; a new building code was introduced, ushering in the construction of reinforced concrete buildings using cement imported in barrels.

1948 The University of the West Indies was founded.

1952 Commercial bauxite mining and alumina production commenced.

1962 Jamaica gained independence.

Notes

Chapter 1

1. C.S. Cotter, "Sevilla Nueva: The Story of an Excavation", *Jamaica Journal* 4, no. 2 (1970): 15–22.
2. R.D. Mathewson, "Archaeological Excavations at Old King's House", *Jamaica Journal* 6, no. 1 (1972): 3–11.
3. R. Coleman, "Olive 'Oyl' and the Eighteenth-Century Royal Navy: An Archaeological Study", in *The Age of Sail: The International Annual of the Historic Sailing Ship,* eds. Nicholas Tracy and Martin Robson (London: Conway Maritime Press, 2003), 2:128–43.
4. Cotter, "Sevilla Nueva".
5. *Journal of the Assembly of Jamaica* [henceforth abbreviated *JAJ*] 8 (1786): 194.
6. Ibid., 248.
7. A.R.D. Porter, T.A. Jackson and E. Robinson, *Minerals and Rocks of Jamaica* (Kingston: Jamaica Publishing House, 1982).
8. Sir Hans Sloane, *A Voyage to the Islands Madera, Barbadoes, Nieves, St. Christophers and Jamaica . . .* (London: B.M. for the author, 1707, 1725), 1:lxvi.
9. C.S. Cotter, "The Discovery of the Spanish Carvings at Seville", *Jamaican Historical Review* 1, no. 3 (1948): 227–34.
10. N.W. Kaye, "Sevilla, First Capital of Jamaica", *West Indian Review* 4, no. 11 (1938): 29–32; "Spanish Stones from New Seville, Jamaica", *Jamaica Journal* 12, no. 43 (1980): 104–6 and back cover.
11. Mathewson, "Archaeological Excavations".
12. A. Hodges, "Lime and Earth: Jamaican Traditional Building Materials and Techniques", *Jamaica Journal* 20, no. 1 (1987): 2–9.

13. M. Williams, *The Slate Industry* (Buckinghamshire: Shire Publications, 1998), 26.

14. C. Nunes, "St Peter's Church, Alley, Clarendon", *Bulletin of the Jamaican Historical Society* 11, no. 7 (2001): 168–70.

15. Alec Henderson, personal communication, 2001.

16. Porter, Jackson and Robinson, *Minerals and Rocks of Jamaica*.

17. J.E. Duerden, "Aboriginal Indian Remains in Jamaica", *Journal of the Institute of Jamaica* 2, no. 4 (1897): 32.

18. M.J. Roobol and J.W. Lee, "Petrography and Source of Some Arawak Rock Artifacts from Jamaica" (paper presented at the Sixth Congrès Internacional pour l'Étude des Cultures Pre-Columbiennes des Petites Antilles, Guadeloupe, 1975), 304–13.

19. *JAJ* 8 (1784): 40.

Chapter 2

1. S. Donovan and T.A. Jackson, "Field Guide to the Geology of the University of the West Indies Campus, Mona", *Caribbean Journal of Earth Science* 34 (2000): 17–24.

2. S. Francis-Brown, *Mona, Past and Present: The History and Heritage of the Mona Campus, University of the West Indies* (Kingston, Jamaica: University of the West Indies Press, 2004).

3. S.F. Panning, "Windmills in Jamaica circa 1804: Cornwall", *Jamaican Historical Society Bulletin* 11, no. 7 (2001): 171–75, and "Windmills in Jamaica circa 1804: Part 2 (Middlesex)", *Jamaican Historical Society Bulletin* 11, no. 10 (2002): 308–12.

4. E. Long, *History of Jamaica* (London: T. Lowndes, 1774), 2:7.

5. "Old King's House Destroyed by Fire", *Gleaner*, 10 October 1925, 1, 3.

Chapter 3

1. *JAJ* 1 (1692): 142.

2. R.F. Marx, *Pirate Port* (London: Pelham Books, 1968); M. Pawson and D. Buisseret, *Port Royal, Jamaica* (Oxford: Oxford University Press, 1975; Kingston: University of the West Indies Press, 2000); C.V. Black, *Port Royal: A History and Guide* (Kingston: Institute of Jamaica Publications, 1988); J. Cox and O. Cox, *Naval Hospitals of Port Royal, Jamaica,* Architectural Monograph Series, no.1 (Kingston: University of Technology, Jamaica, 1999); M.C. Link, "Exploring the Drowned City of Port Royal", *National Geographic,* February 1960, 151–82; Institute of Jamaica, "The Port Royal Project", *Jamaica Journal* 4, no. 2 (1970): 2–12.

3. T.F. Goreau and K.C. Burke, "Pleistocene and Holocene Geology of the Island Shelf Near Kingston, Jamaica", *Marine Geology* 4 (1966): 207–25.

4. *JAJ* 1 (1663): 1; *Calendar of State Papers* (18 June 1661), item 110, p. 38; *Calendar of State Papers* (28 October 1662), item 375, p. 112; *Calendar of State Papers* (8 November 1662), item 384, p. 113.

5. *JAJ* 1 (1664): 2.

6. P. Mayes, "Port Royal, Jamaica: Excavations 1969–70" (Jamaica National Trust Commission, 1972).

7. A.R.D. Porter, "Port Royal: Its Geological Heritage", *Jamaica Journal* 27, nos. 2–3 (2004): 35–40.

8. R. Powell, letter to William Coventry, 26 July 1679. Coventry Papers, vol. 75, pp. 322–24, microfilm, Longleat House, near Warminster, Wiltshire, England.

9. Powell, letter to William Coventry, 30 July 1679.

10. *JAJ* 1 (1686): 85.

11. *JAJ* 2 (1726): 606.

12. M. Pawson, "Fort Rupert Rediscovered", *Jamaican Historical Society Bulletin* 4 (1968): 311–16.

13. A.R.D. Porter, "Imported and Local Stone Use in Pre-1900 Jamaica", *Jamaican Historical Society Bulletin* 11, nos. 8 and 9 (2001): 232–56.

14. J. Murphy, letter to the *Falmouth Post,* 1859, quoted in Frank Cundall, *Historic Jamaica* (London: West India Committee, 1915), 58–59.

15. *Calendar of State Papers* (23 March 1693), item 209, p. 60.

16. *JAJ* 2 (1725): 535.

17. *JAJ* 4 (1749): 223.

18. Long, *History of Jamaica,* 2:152.

19. S.F. Panning, "Evidence of a Light Railway at Port Royal – circa 1900", *Jamaican Historical Society Bulletin* 11, no. 1 (1998): 19–21.

20. *Calendar of State Papers* (20 September 1722), item 295, pp. 144–46.

21. A.R.D. Porter, "Geo-Heritage Walking Tour of Port Royal", *Programme, Abstracts, and Field Guides,* 43–48 (Geological Society of Jamaica Fiftieth Anniversary Conference, Kingston, Jamaica, December 2005).

Chapter 4

1. *Calendar of State Papers* (2 January 1701), item 5, p. 52.
2. *JAJ* 1 (1702): 231.
3. *JAJ* 3 (1738): 451.
4. *JAJ* 4 (1749): 224.
5. *JAJ* 4 (1754): 471, 479–82.
6. Ibid., 477.
7. F. Cundall, "Historic Sites, Ancient Buildings, and Monuments in Jamaica", *Jamaica Gazette* 32, no. 24 (Supplement), 23 December 1909, 640.
8. *JAJ* 4 (1756): 560.
9. *JAJ* 5 (1759): 142.
10. *JAJ* 5 (1763): 404-5.
11. *JAJ* 7 (1777): 94.
12. Ibid., 46.
13. *JAJ* 7 (1778): 110.
14. *JAJ* 8 (1784): 57.
15. Votes of the House of Assembly, 1808-1809, 98-99.
16. Herbert Brenon, "The Great Picture Is Finished", *Gleaner,* 11 April 1916, 3.
17. Internet Movie Database, "Trivia for *A Daughter of the Gods*", http://www.imdb.com/title/tt0006568/trivia; accessed 13 April 2005.
18. Air photographs by Hunting Aerosurveys, N\Jam\49, scale 1:9000, line 12, nos. 4 to 8.
19. Government of Jamaica, Department of Prisons, "Report of the Treatment of Offenders, April 1952 to March 1953", 1, 2.
20. Government of Jamaica, Department of Prisons, "Report of the Treatment of Offenders, April 1954 to March 1955", 4.
21. A. Webster, "Fort Augusta: Then and Now", *Sunday Gleaner,* 27 January 1957, 6.
22. Government of Jamaica, Department of Prisons, "Report of the Treatment of Offenders, April 1959 to March 1960", 4.

Chapter 5

1. P. Browne, *The Civil and Natural History of Jamaica* (1756; 2nd ed., London: B. White and Son, 1789), 63.
2. Duerden, "Aboriginal Indian Remains", 32.
3. Roobol and Lee, "Some Arawak Rock Artifacts", 304–13.
4. Ibid., 309.
5. Ibid., 312.
6. Ibid., 305.
7. Ronald E. Anderson, personal communication, 2001.
8. Jadeite PDF # 22-1338, JCPDS-International Centre for Diffraction Data, 2003.
9. Sloane, *A Voyage to the Islands,* 2:339.
10. Duerden, "Aboriginal Indian Remains", 32.
11. Roobol and Lee, "Some Arawak Rock Artifacts", 307.
12. http://www.cigem.ca/431; accessed January 2003.
13. S. Voynick, "Guatemalan Jade", *Rock and Gem Magazine,* October 2002, 64–69; B. Jones, "Shades of Jade", *Rock and Gem Magazine,* November 2002, 12–15.
14. F. Ward, "Jade-Stone from Heaven", *National Geographic,* September 1987, 282–316.
15. An X ray diffraction site, http://www.rupestre.net; 8 March 2003.

Chapter 6

1. *JAJ* 7 (1778): 122.
2. *JAJ* 7 (1783): 596.
3. A.R.D. Porter, "The Unique Star of David Bricks", *Jamaican Historical Society Bulletin* 11, nos. 11 and 12 (2003): 345–50.
4. J. Shepard, "Star of David Brick". One-page pamphlet distributed by Swiss Stores, Kingston, Jamaica, 1998.

Chapter 7

1. Roobol and Lee, "Some Arawak Rock Artifacts", 304–13.
2. G. Lechler, "Chancery Hall, St Andrew . . . Taino Site on the Outskirts of Kingston", *Archaeology Jamaica* 12 (2000): 10–11.

3. R. Ahmad, "Is There Opal in Jamaica?" *Geological Society of Jamaica Newsletter* 6, no. 1 (May 1985): 23–24.

4. Sloane, *A Voyage to the Islands,* 1:lxvii.

5. F.J. Osborne, "Spanish Church, St Ann's Bay", *Jamaica Journal* 8 (1971): 33–35.

6. T. Bonner, "Blue Mountains Expedition: Exploratory Excavations at Nanny Town", *Jamaica Journal* 8, nos. 2 and 3 (1974): 46–50.

7. Francis-Brown, *Mona, Past and Present.*

8. Donovan and Jackson, "Geology of the UWI Campus, Mona", 17–24.

9. Sloane, *A Voyage to the Islands,* 1:x–xi.

10. Browne, *Civil and Natural History,* 63–64.

11. E.W. Andrews and C.M. Andrews, eds., *The Journal of a Lady of Quality (Being the Narrative of a Journey from Scotland to the West Indies, North Carolina, and Portugal, in the years 1774 to 1776)* (New Haven: Yale University Press, 1927), 60, 61, 84.

12. Ingrid Blackman, Barbados, letter to the author, 7 January 2000.

13. H.S. Fraser, *Treasures of Barbados* (London: Macmillan, 1990), 17–18.

14. G. Robertson, "Dripstones", *Jamaican Historical Society Bulletin* 5, nos. 6 and 7 (1990): 100.

15. K.J. Mesolella, "The Uplifted Reefs of Barbados: Physical Stratigraphy, Facies Relationships and Absolute Chronology" (PhD thesis, Brown University, 1968).

16. M. Stanbury and I.D. MacLeod, "Colonies, Convicts, and Filtering Stones: Roads to Solutions", *Bulletin of the Australian Institute for Maritime Archaeology* 12, no. 2 (1989): 1–10.

17. R.A. Coleman, "Dripstones: Rudimentary Water Filters on Ship and Shore in the Eighteenth Century", *Bulletin of the Australian Institute for Maritime Archaeology* 25 (2001): 113–20.

18. S.B.J. Skertchly, *Manufacture of Gun-flints, Etc. Memoirs of the Geological Survey, England and Wales* (1879; reprint [limited edition], Bloomfield, Ont.: Museum Restoration Services, 1984.

19. *JAJ* 1 (1701): 228.

20. *JAJ* 13 (1816): 20.

21. Duerden, "Aboriginal Indian Remains", 7, 37.

22. Porter, "Imported and Local Stone", 232–56.

23. Duerden, "Aboriginal Indian Remains", 37.

24. Fraser, *Treasures of Barbados,* 17, 18.

25. Porter, "Imported and Local Stone", 232–56.

Glossary

Note: The glossary includes terms used in illustrations as well as in the text.

American bond. A masonry bond in which the headers are laid every fourth, fifth or sixth course.

amulet. An item worn to protect against evil (such as disease or witchcraft) or to otherwise aid the wearer.

arch bridge. A bridge in which the spans or main supporting elements each form an arch.

ashlar. Rectangular or squared stone.

ashlar facing. Sawed or dressed squared stones used in facing masonry walls.

ashlar masonry. Masonry made of dressed, sawed, tooled or quarried stone with a proper bond.

ballast. A relatively heavy substance used to maintain a ship at its proper draft or trim, or to improve its stability (such as rock stowed in holds or water in tanks).

banquette. A ledge, step or raised platform along the inside of a parapet (or trench), for soldiers to stand on when firing upon the enemy.

bastion. A projecting (often four-sided) part of a fortification consisting of two faces and two flanks. The two faces form an acute angle called the salient angle that commands the land or water in front of it, while each flank commands and defends the adjacent curtain (or that portion of the wall extending from one bastion to another). The distance between the two flanks is known as the gorge, or entrance into the bastion.

Bath stone. A creamy limestone found near Bath, very easily quarried and used in England for building purposes since the twelfth century.

battlement. A parapet on top of a wall, consisting of a series of regularly spaced uprights called merlons alternating with open spaces called crenels (crenelles) or embrasures. It is constructed for defensive purposes or decoration. In the Middle Ages the crenels were narrowed and the sides often splayed (that is, slanted outwards).

breastwork. A temporary fortification.

brick. A substance made chiefly from clay moulded into oblong blocks and baked or burned in a kiln or by the sun. Used in the construction of buildings and walls.

bauxite. An ore containing large amounts of hydrated aluminium oxide, from which almost all the world's aluminium is obtained. Bauxite is named for the town of Les Baux in France, where it was discovered in 1821. Jamaican bauxite is friable and earthy, but in many other countries it is hard and rocklike.

calcarenite. A sedimentary rock composed of sand-sized grains of calcium carbonate. Also referred to as carbonate sand.

capstone. A crowning stone at the summit of a wall, turret, tower or other structure; or any of a series of flat slabs placed on top of a wall to protect its joints.

casemate. A fortified position in a fort or rampart with an opening through which cannon or other guns may be fired. Also, a chamber or armoured enclosure on a warship from which guns are fired.

cement. A finely ground powder containing about 60 per cent lime, 25 per cent silica and 5 per cent alumina (as shale), plus gypsum and iron oxide, that sets to a hard mass when mixed with water. Also known as Portland cement.

chalcedony. A microcrystalline variety of quartz (silicon dioxide). It is usually pale blue or green to grey, has a waxy lustre and cannot be scratched by a knife blade.

chert. An opaque, whitish to pale brown or grey, very fine-grained variety of quartz. It frequently occurs as nodules or beds in limestone (notably the Montpelier Formation in Jamaica). Contrast **flint**.

chevaux-de-frise. A protecting line of sharp points (such as spikes or nails) firmly set into the top of a fence or wall.

concrete. A mixture of cement, sand and a coarse, chemically inert particulate matter called aggregate (generally not exceeding 1 inch or 2.54 centimetres in size) that hardens when mixed with water.

copestone. The top stone of a wall or building.

coping. The highest or covering course of a wall, usually with a slanted or sloping top to carry off water.

coping stone. Any stone used as a coping.

cordon. A line or circle guarding an area.

cornice. A horizontal moulding that projects along the top of a wall, building or entablature; also, the decorative strip above a window that shields a curtain rod from view.

course. A continuous level or horizontal layer of brick or masonry, capping or constituting the body of a wall.

coursed ashlar. Masonry in which the stones in a course are essentially the same height.

coursed rubble. Masonry composed of roughly shaped stones fitting approximately on level beds.

covert-way. A secret hiding or sheltered place.

crenel. A notch or squared indentation at the top of a battlement or wall; an embrasure. The sides of crenels through which cannons are fired are often splayed (spread outward) to provide a greater arc for the guns to swing through.

curtain. A stretch of wall that connects two neighbouring bastions. It serves to enclose rather than to support.

damp-proof course. A course of some impermeable material laid on the foundation walls of a building, a short distance above ground level, to prevent moisture from rising up the walls.

date stone. A stone marked or inscribed with the date when an event occurred.

dentil. An architectural term applied to one of a series of small ornamental rectangular blocks arranged like a row of teeth on the side of a building, as, for example, under a cornice.

dripstone. Naturally formed deposits of calcium carbonate, precipitated largely in caves from dripping water; also, man-made receptacles, carved out of porous rock or stone, for filtering water.

embrasure. An open space in a wall between two merlons, through which cannons are fired. Also called a crenel.

emery. A dark-grey to black, very hard, fine-grained magnetic rock composed of corundum (Al_2O_3), magnetite and, less commonly, spinel. It has long been used to cut, grind and polish rocks and ornamental stones.

English bond. A masonry bond in which courses of headers and stretchers alternate.

extrados. The outer curve of an arch.

felsite. A geological term for any light-coloured, very fine-grained igneous rock with or without phenocrysts and composed chiefly of quartz and feldspar.

flagstone. A hard sandstone, usually micaceous and fine-grained, that occurs in extensive thin beds with shale partings; it splits uniformly along bedding planes into thin slabs suitable for use in terrace floors, retaining walls and so on; also, a flat slab of stone used for paving.

Flemish bond. A masonry bond in which the headers and stretchers alternate in the same course.

flint. A very fine-grained variety of quartz, characterized by its dark-grey to black colour, opaque lustre (except in thin slices, which are translucent brown), hardness and conchoidal fracture. Contrast **chert**.

freestone. Any stone, especially a thick-bedded limestone or a sandstone, that breaks freely and can be cut and dressed in any direction without splitting. See also Bath stone.

frieze. In architecture, a horizontal band, usually decorated with sculptures, situated between the architrave and cornice of a building.

gallet; galleting. A chip of stone; the technique of infilling fresh mortar joints with gallets.

glacis. A gently sloping bank in front of a counterscarp that shields the ditch from enemy fire and exposes the enemy advancing up the slope to the most direct line of fire from the fort.

gorge. See bastion.

granite. A common igneous rock composed mainly of large visible crystals of quartz, feldspar and mica. It is hard, durable and used extensively as a building stone.

greenstone. A field term for any compact, dark-green, altered or metamorphosed basic igneous rock that owes its colour to chlorite, actinolite or epidote.

grindstone. A flat, circular piece of natural sandstone that revolves on an axle and is used for grinding tools or for shaping or smoothing objects; also, a millstone.

gritstone. (British) A hard, coarse-grained siliceous sandstone.

gun carriage. A mechanical structure upon which a gun is mounted for manoeuvring, firing and being transported.

gun flint. The piece of flint that is placed in a gunlock and which produces the spark that ignites the gunpowder.

header. The short end of a brick. A masonry bond consisting of courses faced with headers is called a header bond.

hexagram. A six-pointed, star-shaped figure formed by two intersecting equilateral triangles.

hogshead. A large wooden barrel or cask of variable capacity used in colonial times to measure, store and transport sugar, molasses, tobacco, wine and other commodities.

intrados. The inner curve of an arch.

keystone. The uppermost or central stone of an arch or vault, wider at the top than at the bottom; being placed last, it fits like a wedge that binds or holds the other arch-stones (or *voussoirs*) together. It may project outwards and be ornamented.

lime. Calcium oxide (CaO), a white substance obtained from burning limestone ($CaCO_3$). It is used in mortar and cement, for painting and to neutralize acidic soil, among other uses.

limestone. A sedimentary rock composed entirely or chiefly of calcium carbonate, widely used for construction purposes and making lime. When it contains magnesium carbonate it is called dolomitic limestone. When altered by intense heat and pressure, it is transformed into marble.

lintel. A horizontal architectural unit that spans an opening and carries the load both above and below.

loophole. A small opening in a wall, used for observation or discharging small arms.

mano. A hand-held grinding stone (also called a handstone, roller or muller).

merlon. The upright part of a battlement (or embattled parapet) between two crenels or embrasures.

metate. A stone block with a shallow concave surface, used in conjunction with a mano to grind seeds, nuts and grains. Also referred to as abraders or mealing stones. Other types, manufactured in Central and South America, are carved out of granite and other stone types and are characterized by flat surfaces supported by three legs – hence the name "tripod metate".

millstone. One of a pair of flat, round stones used for grinding grain into flour. The lower stone, called the bed stone, is stationary, while the other, called the runner stone, rotates in a horizontal plane above the bed stone. Both have master grooves (channels) which run from a central hole, or eye, from the rotating shaft to the outer edge of the stone.

mortar. A strong bowl in which substances may be broken or pulverized to a powder with a pestle; also, a mixture of cement or lime, sand or crushed stone (less than 4.8 millimetres), and water. It is used for binding bricks, blocks and stones, usually in walls, and for rendering surfaces.

musket. A gun with a long barrel and a smooth bore, introduced in the 1500s and widely used before the development of the rifle.

oolitic. A term used to describe rocks, predominantly limestone, composed mainly of many small, rounded bodies (ooliths) resembling fish eggs, with a diameter of 0.25 to 2.0 millimetres. Each oolith is formed by the gradual accretion of mineral matter in concentric layers around a nucleus, such as a particle of sand.

orillon. An archaic term meaning a projection, built out at the corner of a bastion between flank and face, from which to defend the flank.

palisade. A fence or row of stakes set firmly in the ground to enclose an area or provide protection against an enemy.

palladian. An architectural unit consisting of a central window with an arched head, flanked on each side by a narrower window with a square head.

palmetto piles. Wooden logs derived from various palms with fan-shaped leaves, such as the cabbage palm (*Roystonea oleracea*).

parapet. A wall of earth or stone placed around the edge of a fort top, or other structure, to conceal and protect soldiers from frontal enemy attack; also, a low wall on a roof, balcony or the sides of a bridge.

phenocryst. A prominent, often rectangular-shaped crystal in an igneous rock that is larger than the matrix in which it is embedded

pictograph. An ancient drawing or painting on a rock – for example, on the face of a cliff or on the wall of a cave.

pigeon wood piles. Wooden logs derived from various tropical trees with marked or mottled wood (*Diospyros tetrasperma*).

plinth. The square block at the base of a column, pedestal or similar structure.

point. To fill joints in brickwork with cement or mortar.

quoin. The stone, brick or wood that forms the external corner of a building.

rampart. A defensive wall or embankment, usually with a battlement at its top.

ravelin. A detached outwork in a fortification, with two faces that project outward and form a salient angle, constructed beyond the main ditch and in front of the curtain.

redoubt. A small, enclosed defensive work, usually temporary, that is used to fortify a strategic position.

relief. A work of art consisting of sculpted figures or forms that are higher than the background.

rowlock arch. An arch in which the voussoirs (archstones) are arranged in separate concentric rings.

rubble. Masonry composed largely of rubble stone (stones and bricks of any shape).

salient angle. An angle in a fortification that projects outwards (see bastion) or in a battle line with its apex towards the enemy.

sally port. A large gate or passage in a fortified place, used by troops to make an exit or to engage the enemy.

schooner. A sailing ship with two or more masts, rigged with fore-and-aft sails.

serrated course. A single layer of bricks below the covering course, one corner edge of which forms a zigzag or sawtooth pattern and overhangs the course below. This design is conspicuous and decorative, but it serves to keep water away from the course below.

slate. A hard, very fine-grained metamorphic rock that splits naturally into thin, smooth-surfaced layers. It was at one time extensively used as a roofing tile and as a tablet for writing on with chalk.

specific gravity. The ratio of the weight of a given volume of a substance to the weight of an equal volume of water. Various balances have been designed to measure the specific gravity of minerals and gems.

stretcher. The long side (or face) of a brick.

tackle. An arrangement of pulleys and ropes used for pulling or raising heavy objects.

tailing. The projecting part of a brick or stone that is inserted into a wall.

terra cotta. Baked (literally, cooked) earth or clay.

terreplein. In fortifications, a platform or horizontal surface behind a rampart, on which guns are placed and fired.

tessellate. A checkered design or appearance.

texture. Refers to the size, shape, arrangement and distribution of minerals that make up a rock.

Triassic. The geologic period extending from 225 to 190 million years ago.

turret. A small tower, built for military or decorative purposes, at the angle of a wall.

vault. An arched ceiling, roof or covering of masonry; also, an underground arched chamber. In architecture, a single vault, semi-cylindrical in cross-section, with two parallel abutments, is referred to as a barrel, tunnel or wagon vault.

voussoir. One of the tapering or truncated wedge-shaped pieces of stone or brick forming an arch or vault.

whetstone. An abrasive stone (usually fine-grained and siliceous) suitable for sharpening implements.

X-ray diffraction. The deflection of a beam of electromagnetic radiation (called X-rays) by the regularly spaced atoms in a crystalline material.

XRF. An abbreviation for "X-ray fluorescence", a method used by scientists to determine the elemental composition of a substance, expressed as per cent oxides.

Selected Bibliography

Ahmad, R. "Is There Opal in Jamaica?" *Geological Society of Jamaica Newsletter* 6, no. 1 (May 1985): 23–24.

Andrews, E.W., and C.M. Andrews, eds. *The Journal of a Lady of Quality (Being the Narrative of a Journey from Scotland to the West Indies, North Carolina, and Portugal, in the years 1774 to 1776).* New Haven: Yale University Press, 1927.

Black, C.V. *Port Royal: A History and Guide.* Kingston: Institute of Jamaica Publications, 1988.

Bonner, T. "Blue Mountains Expedition: Exploratory Excavations at Nanny Town". *Jamaica Journal* 8, nos. 2 and 3 (1974), 46–50.

Browne, P. *The Civil and Natural History of Jamaica,* 2nd ed. London: B. White and Son, 1789.

Coleman, R.A. "Dripstones: Rudimentary Water Filters on Ship and Shore in the Eighteenth Century". *Bulletin of the Australian Institute for Maritime Archaeology* 25 (2001): 113–20.

———. "Olive 'Oyl' and the Eighteenth-Century Royal Navy: An Archaeological Study". In *The Age of Sail: The International Annual of the Historic Sailing Ship.* Vol. 2. Edited by Nicholas Tracy and Martin Robson, 128–43. London: Conway Maritime Press, 2003.

Cotter, C.S. "The Discovery of the Spanish Carvings at Seville". *Jamaican Historical Review* 1, no. 3 (1948): 227–34.

———. "Sevilla Nueva: The Story of an Excavation". *Jamaica Journal* 4, no. 2 (1970): 15–22.

Cox, J., and O. Cox. *Naval Hospitals of Port Royal, Jamaica.* Architectural Monograph Series, no. 1. Kingston: University of Technology, Jamaica, 1999.

Cundall, F. *Historic Jamaica.* Published for the Institute of Jamaica. London: West India Committee, 1915.

———. "Historic Sites, Ancient Buildings, and Monuments in Jamaica". *Jamaica Gazette* 32, no. 24 (Supplement), 23 December 1909, 640.

Donovan, S., and T.A. Jackson. "Field Guide to the Geology of the University of the West Indies Campus, Mona". *Caribbean Journal of Earth Science* 34 (2000): 17–24.

Duerden, J.E. "Aboriginal Indian Remains in Jamaica". *Journal of the Institute of Jamaica* 2, no. 4 (1897): 32.

Francis-Brown, S. *Mona, Past and Present: The History and Heritage of the Mona Campus, University of the West Indies.* Kingston: University of the West Indies Press, 2004.

Fraser, H.S. *Treasures of Barbados.* London: Macmillan, 1990.

Goreau, T.F., and K.C. Burke. "Pleistocene and Holocene Geology of the Island Shelf near Kingston, Jamaica". *Marine Geology* 4 (1966): 207–25.

Hodges, A. "Lime and Earth: Jamaican Traditional Building Materials and Techniques". *Jamaica Journal* 20, no. 1 (1987): 2–9.

Institute of Jamaica. "The Port Royal Project". *Jamaica Journal* 4, no. 2 (1970): 2–12.

———. "Spanish Stones from New Seville, Jamaica". *Jamaica Journal* 12, no. 43 (1980): 104–6, back cover.

Jones, B. "Shades of Jade". *Rock and Gem Magazine.* November 2002, 12–15.

Kaye, N.W. "Sevilla, First Capital of Jamaica". *West Indian Review* 4, no. 11 (1938): 29–32.

Lechler, G. "Chancery Hall, St Andrew . . . Taino Site on the Outskirts of Kingston". *Archaeology Jamaica* 12 (2000): 10–11.

Link, M.C. "Exploring the Drowned City of Port Royal". *National Geographic.* February 1960, 151–82.

Long, E. *History of Jamaica.* 2 vols. London: T. Lowndes, 1774.

Marx, R.F. *Pirate Port.* London: Pelham Books, 1968.

Mathewson, R.D. "Archaeological Excavations at Old King's House". *Jamaica Journal* 6, no. 1 (1972): 3–11.

Mayes, P. "Port Royal, Jamaica: Excavations 1969–70". Jamaica National Trust Commission, 1972.

Mesolella, K.J. "The Uplifted Reefs of Barbados: Physical Stratigraphy, Facies Relationships and Absolute Chronology". PhD thesis, Brown University, 1968.

Nunes, C. "St Peter's Church, Alley, Clarendon". *Bulletin of the Jamaican Historical Society* 11, no. 7 (2001): 168–70.

Osborne, F.J. "Spanish Church, St Ann's Bay". *Jamaica Journal* 8 (1971): 33–35.

Panning, S.F. "Evidence of a Light Railway at Port Royal – circa 1900". *Jamaican Historical Society Bulletin* 11, no. 1 (1998): 19–21.

———. "Windmills in Jamaica circa 1804: Cornwall". *Jamaican Historical Society Bulletin* 11, no. 7 (2001): 171–75

———. "Windmills in Jamaica circa 1804: Part 2 (Middlesex)". *Jamaican Historical Society Bulletin* 11, no. 10 (2002): 308–12.

Pawson, M. "Fort Rupert Rediscovered". *Jamaican Historical Society Bulletin* 4 (1968): 311–16.

Pawson, M., and D. Buisseret. *Port Royal, Jamaica.* Oxford: Oxford University Press, 1975; Kingston: University of the West Indies Press, 2000.

Porter, A.R.D. "Imported and Local Stone Use in Pre-1900 Jamaica". *Jamaican Historical Society Bulletin* 11, nos. 8 and 9 (2001): 232–56.

———. "Port Royal: Its Geological Heritage". *Jamaica Journal* 27, nos. 2–3 (2004): 35–40.

———. "The Unique Star of David Bricks". *Jamaican Historical Society Bulletin* 11, nos. 11 and 12 (2003): 345–50.

Porter, A.R.D., T.A. Jackson and E. Robinson. *Minerals and Rocks of Jamaica.* Kingston: Jamaica Publishing House, 1982.

———. Jamaica: A Geological Portrait. Kingston: Institute of Jamaica Publications, 1990.

Robertson, G. "Dripstones". *Jamaican Historical Society Bulletin* 5, nos. 6 and 7 (1990): 100.

Roobol, M.J., and J.W. Lee. "Petrography and Source of Some Arawak Rock Artifacts from Jamaica". Paper presented at the Sixth Congrès Internacional pour l'Étude des Cultures Pre-Columbiennes des Petites Antilles, Guadeloupe, 1975.

Skertchly, S.B.J. *Manufacture of Gun-flints, Etc. Memoirs of the Geological Survey, England and Wales.* 1879. Rpt., Bloomfield, Ont.: Museum Restoration Services, 1984.

Sloane, Sir Hans. *A Voyage to the Islands Madera, Barbadoes, Nieves, St. Christophers and Jamaica . . .* 2 vols. London: B.M. for the author, 1707, 1725.

Stanbury, M., and I.D. MacLeod. "Colonies, Convicts, and Filtering Stones: Roads to Solutions". *Bulletin of the Australian Institute for Maritime Archaeology* 12, no. 2 (1989): 1–10.

Voynick, S. "Guatemalan Jade". *Rock and Gem Magazine.* October 2002, 64–69.

Ward, F. "Jade-Stone from Heaven". *National Geographic.* September 1987, 282–316.

Williams, M. *The Slate Industry.* Buckinghamshire: Shire Publications, 1998.

Index